C owley Publications is a ministry of the brothers of the Society of Saint John the Evangelist, a monastic order in the Episcopal Church. Our mission is to provide books and resources for those seeking spiritual and theological formation. Cowley Publications is committed to developing a new generation of writers and teachers who will encourage people to think and pray in new ways about spirituality, reconciliation, and the future.

Get Up Off Your Knees

Preaching the U2 Catalog

Raewynne J. Whiteley and Beth Maynard, editors

Cowley Publications

Cambridge, Massachusetts

Published in the United States of America by Cowley Publications, a division of the Society of Saint John the Evangelist. No portion of this book may be reproduced, stored in or introduced into a retrieval system, or transmitted, in any form or by any means—including photocopying—without the prior written permission of Cowley Publications, except in the case of brief quotations embedded in critical articles and reviews.

Library of Congress Cataloging-in-Publication Data

Get up off your knees : preaching the U2 catalog / Raewynne J. Whiteley and Beth Maynard, editors.
    p.cm.
Includes bibliographical references.
ISBN 1-56101-223-8 (pbk. : alk. paper)
1. Sermons, English—21st century. 2. U2 (Musical group) 3. Rock music—Religious aspects—Christianity—Sermons. 4. Bible—Sermons. I. Whiteley, Raewynne J., 1966- II. Maynard, Beth, 1962–
BV4241.G48 2003
252—dc22
                    2003021239

U2 Music and Lyrics published by Blue Mountain Music Ltd. (for the UK)/Mother Music Ltd. (for the Republic of Ireland)/Universal Music.

Publishing BV (For The Rest Of The World) U2 Recordings owned by Universal International Music B.V. exclusively licensed to Island Records (ROW) and Interscope Records (USA).

Unless indicated otherwise, scripture quotations are taken from *The New Revised Standard Version of the Bible,* © 1989, by the Division of Christian Education of the National Council of the Churches of Christ in the United States of America. Used by permission.

Cover photo: Otto Kitsinger   Cover design: Gary Ragaglia

This book was by Transcontinental Printing in Canada.

Cowley Publications
907 Massachusetts Avenue
Cambridge, Massachusetts 02139
800-225-1534 • www.cowley.org

The royalties from this book will go to support The AIDS Support Organization (TASO) in Uganda. Suggested to us by DATA and Principle Management New York, TASO serves the poorest sections of society with education, support, and direct care. It provides food and medicine, promotes avoidance of risky behaviors, and works to end discrimination against people living with AIDS. TASO is recognized around the world as a leader in providing innovative, affordable programs, and has played a major role in reducing AIDS prevalence rates in Uganda from 15 percent of adults ten years ago to just 5 percent today. Visit TASO on the web at www.tasouganda.org.

The Editors

Contents

ix Acknowledgements

xi Foreword by Eugene H. Peterson

xv Introduction by Raewynne J. Whiteley and Beth Maynard

1 Part 1: october/new year's day by Sarah Dylan Breuer

3 There's a heaviness in the air . . .
by Raewynne J. Whiteley

9 To See What You See: On Liturgy & Learning & Life
by Steven Garber

15 Not Afraid to Die, Not Afraid to Live
by Henry VanderSpek

23 Temples of an Incarnate God by David Friedrich

27 Part 2: until the end of the world by Sarah Dylan Breuer

31 The Psalms, the Blues, and the Telling of Truth
by Jamie Howison

37 Wake Up Dead Man: Singing the Psalms of Lament
by Brian J. Walsh

43 Deliverance Where the Streets Have No Name
by Stephen Butler Murray

49 Bridging the Betweens by Raewynne J. Whiteley

53 Part 3: staring at the sun by Sarah Dylan Breuer

55 Reconcilers in a Violent World by Jay R. Lawlor

61 Grace: U2, the Apostle Paul, and Latin American
Theology by Clint McCann

69 Living the Question: Privilege, Poverty, and Faith
by Jennifer M. McBride

75 Walk On: Biblical Hope and U2 by Brian J. Walsh

83   Part 4: desire by Sarah Dylan Breuer
85   Pressing On with U2 and Paul by Steve Stockman
91   Beyond Prosperity by Jamie Parsley
95   Finding The Way To The Playboy Mansion
      by Derek Walmsley
99   Wandering Sheep by Darleen Pryds
103   If We Were More Like Thomas by Beth Maynard

109   Part 5: elevation by Sarah Dylan Breuer
111   The Coming of Love by Julie Bogart
115   A Wedding Sermon for Nathan and Sandie
      by Steven Garber
121   The Voice You Find May Be Your Own
      by Anna Carter Florence
127   Love's Dim Reflection by Shawnthea Monroe-Mueller

131   Part 6: fire by Sarah Dylan Breuer
133   Lent, Part One by Beth Maynard
139   Grace the Beauty-Maker by Wade Hodges
145   Dying to Live by Leslie J. Reinke
149   A Turning Point by Amy Lincoln
153   An Army of One by Mike Kinman

Appendices
157   A: "Woo me, sister; move me, brother!" What does
      Pop Culture Have to Do with Preaching?
      by Raewynne J. Whiteley
167   B: A Brief History of U2 for Novices by Beth Maynard
177   C: Pursuing God with U2: An Adult Study
      by Beth Maynard

205   Contributors

Acknowledgments

With thanks to:
My brother, John, who kept playing U2 when I was awash in Bach and Bartok, and who has kept me listening to their music with gifts of CDs—and demands that preaching have something to do with real life;
Bishop Penny Jamieson, who cooked me a great meal one night, and that same night encouraged me to follow my dream of a PhD—and in so doing helped me to find my voice; and to God, for the incredible gift of preaching, without which I cannot imagine living.

Raewynne J. Whiteley

These two individuals would probably be very surprised to find me thanking them:
Gwen Prestwood, who handed me her copy of *The Joshua Tree* one night in 1987, and Tony Campbell, God rest his soul, who asked me one afternoon in 1991, "Are you a preacher?"
I'm also grateful to the U2 fandom, whose conviction, generosity, and intelligence usually outweigh their tendency to take themselves too seriously, and who have made me ask questions I never imagined asking about the shape of faithful living. Without U2, my spiritual life would have a much less interesting soundtrack. Without Jesus, I'd probably be either intolerable or dead.

Beth Maynard

Foreword

A friend recently invited some of his friends to invite all the friends they knew who loved the songs of U2 for an evening of "Jesus and Bono." Most of the people gathered were not followers of Jesus—they would have been embarrassed to be identified that way—but they were unembarrassed followers of U2. Bono had gotten their attention. *More* than their attention. Bono had engaged them at some level of spirit more authentic than the culture of addictions and consumerism they were accustomed to living in. They seemed pleased to be included in considering Bono in the company of Jesus.

It turned out to be an interesting evening. The followers of U2 found themselves comfortable in the company of Jesus and the whore at Simon the Pharisee's supper table (Lk. 7). They were surprised to find that U2 is only following in the footsteps and words of Jesus in their criticism of tele-religion and commercialized god-talk (Mt. 23). They didn't know that U2's outrage over our American complacent indifference to poverty and suffering and injustice, and their determined passion to do something about it, have their origins in Jesus' outrage over a similar calloused complacency in the society in which he lived (Mt. 25). They had no idea that the biblical psalms that Jesus prayed are models for the sometimes angry, sometimes sad, often prayerful lyrics in many of U2's songs.

Is U2 a prophetic voice? I rather think so. And many of my friends think so. If they do not explicitly proclaim the Kingdom, they certainly prepare the way for that proclamation in much the same way that John the Baptist prepared the way for the kerygma of Jesus.

• • •

One of the maddeningly enduring habits of the human race is to insist on domesticating God. We are determined to tame God. We figure out ways to harness God to our projects. We try to reduce God to a size that conveniently fits our plans and ambitions and tastes. We are pleased when we find that there are men and women coming alongside us, offering a rendition of gods or goddesses that give us what we want when we want it and on our own terms. Publicists and propagandists, joined by a surprising number of leading religious figures, are among this company. They cannily manipulate our hunger for meaning and mystery to sell us their product or enlist us in their cause. They are masters at using some so-called "spirituality" as a ruse for exploiting our anxieties and hormones.

And then a prophet shows up and tells us that we can't do it. We can't fit God into our plans, we must fit into his. We can't use God—God is not a tool or appliance or credit card. Prophets confront us with the sovereign presence of God in our lives. If we won't face up, they grab us by the scruff of our necks and shake us into attention. Amos crafted poems, Jeremiah wept sermons, Isaiah alternately rebuked and comforted, Ezekiel did street theater. U2 writes songs and goes on tour, singing them.

• • •

Prophets are characteristically masters of metaphor. Metaphor is the witness of language to the interconnectedness of all things visible and invisible. A metaphor takes a word that is commonly used to refer to a thing or action that we experience by means of our five senses and then uses it to refer to something that is beyond the reach of our immediate senses. "Rock," for instance, refers to a hard mass of minerals that can be held and weighed and seen and painted. It designates what I stub my toe on or throw through a window. There is no ambiguity in the word. It stays the same no matter what. And then one day Jesus looks at Simon and says,

"You are a rock." What was that supposed to mean? By means of the miracle of metaphor, the word, taking the man with it, was launched into another realm of meaning altogether. Simon has been Rock (Peter, *petros*) ever since. We are still trying to figure out all the connections and implications set in motion by that metaphor.

At the simplest level, words identify things or actions. The word is a label. But when used as a metaphor, a word explodes into life—it starts *moving*. I imagine myself entering a museum where every exhibit is identified by a word or words. The exhibits of animals and birds and artifacts are fascinating—there is so much to know! I observe and read and learn. And then suddenly, without warning, the birds are flying. The animals are running and growling and hunting for their supper. The women in the exhibits are trying on Egyptian gold necklaces and competing for attention while the men grab Greek javelins and go into combat. The place is no longer a museum in which I can study or admire inert things; it is a world teeming with life and movement and action in which I am a participant—dodging the animals, admiring the women, avoiding the javelins—whether I want to or not.

Metaphor does that, makes me a participant in creating the meaning and entering into the action of the word. I can no longer understand the word by looking it up in the dictionary for it is no longer just itself; it is alive and moving, inviting me to participate in the meaning. When prophets use metaphor, we get involved with God whether we want to or not, sometimes whether we know it or not.

When metaphor is banished and language is bullied into serving as mere information and definition, as happens so often in our computerized culture and cultural religion, the life goes out of the language. It also goes out of us. When this reduction happens in relation to God and all that pertains to God, we end up sitting around having study and discussion groups in religious museums. If we are lucky, a prophet, one of the descendants of Hosea or Jonah or Habakkuk, shows up and with the simple expedient of a metaphor, said or sung, drags us outside into the open air where all the stuff we are studying is alive and moving and colliding with us. For many these days, it is U2 that shows up.

• • •

In retrospect it comes as no surprise that substantial elements of the Christian church have responded to U2 with something less than enthusiasm, responses ranging from wary detachment to condescension to outright rejection. For even though three members of the band are candid and unqualified in their witness as followers of Jesus, they have little patience with media-driven aspects of the Christian religion and a church and culture that shows little concern for justice and poverty and sickness, especially the out-of-control epidemic of AIDS in Africa. In every age, religion has served as a convenient cover among an astonishing number of people for cozy self-righteousness and a judgmental rejection of suffering sinners. Prophetic voices that challenge the people of God to live "in accordance with the scriptures," scriptures that are especially vocal about care for the poor, the suffering, and the disreputable, have never received cordial treatment from people who use religion to cocoon themselves from reality.

What prophets do, the good ones, is purge our imaginations of the culture's assumptions on what counts in life and how life is lived. Over and over again, God the Holy Spirit has used prophets, biblical and contemporary, to separate people from the lies and illusions to which they've become accustomed and put them back on the path of simple faith and obedience and worship in defiance of all that the world admires and rewards. Prophets train us in discerning the difference between the ways of the world and the ways of the Gospel, keeping us present to the Presence of God.

In the pages that follow, some of my friends welcome U2 into the company of prophetic voices that through the centuries have prepared the way of the Lord, the same Lord Jesus whose Gospel we are responsible for preaching and teaching.

Eugene H. Peterson
Professor Emeritus of Spiritual Theology
Regent College, Vancouver, B.C., Canada

Introduction

Raewynne J. Whiteley and Beth Maynard

I t all started in a chapel in St. Louis, an evening service, populated largely by college students. It was December 2001, and our TV screens were full of news of war in Afghanistan, suicide bombings in Israel, and military action in the West Bank. The searing images of September 11 were not far from our minds. And Christmas carols played in the stores, and decorations decked the streets: Christmas was coming, welcome or not.

The guest preacher that evening was one of us—Raewynne Whiteley—who was in town for a conference, where she presented a paper using a U2 song to talk about the relationship between preaching, GenX, and pop culture. And as she read the text of the day, from Isaiah 53, the words of U2's "Peace on Earth" ran through her brain. They seemed to catch the essential ambivalence of the season. And so for the second time that weekend Raewynne drew on U2's work, now to create the sermon which appears in this book as "Bridging the Betweens."

After the service, the chaplain, Mike Kinman, and Raewynne talked about the significance of U2 in their own spiritual journeys and in the spirituality of the communities in which they worship—and how often U2 lyrics came to mind when they were preparing sermons, an experience they shared with Beth Maynard. Once all three of us were in conversation about the topic, it just seemed obvious: There must be so many other preachers who feel this way. It was a short step from there to the idea of a collection of sermons which draw on the music of U2. And with Cowley Publications on board, Beth and Raewynne began to work on turning the dream into reality (Mike had to move on to other things— thanks for all your help, Mike!).

In November 2002, we put out a call for sermons. And the response was awesome. Submissions came to us from all over, a fascinating and eclectic mix of works by lay Christians, chaplains, academics, and parish clergy. Most of the contributors were under 40, but older preachers had much to say as well. People whose knowledge of the band was fairly limited sat side by side with those who had been dedicated fans since the early 1980s. And several different theological tribes were represented, ranging from Roman Catholic to Irish Presbyterian, from independent evangelical to Episcopalian and back. We've tried to reflect this diversity, as well as the breadth within U2's catalog, in the sermons selected.

We expect our readers to be equally diverse. Some may hope these sermons will teach them more about God, while others are here to learn more about U2. Some fans may come to this collection with the suspicion that it's yet one more example of the institutional church trying to twist and hijack U2 for its own agenda. Some church leaders may want to use the book as a way of getting their feet wet in the concept that popular culture is a prime locus for theological reflection for a large swath of the Western world. We hope there is something here for all these perspectives and more, as well as for different learning styles, since we've included an adult education curriculum, meditations, and essays along with the sermons themselves.

We have tried to be clear from the beginning that the focus of this anthology is not in the members of U2 as individuals, what they believe, or how they question. The focus is their music, and how that music goads and invites preachers into seeing Gospel ideas through a new lens and proclaiming them afresh. We have no illusion that the way songs are used in these sermons constitutes what they "really mean." In fact, we read some of the songs differently than our contributors do, and most U2 texts have at least a double meaning anyway. We simply trust that the music is big enough to leave room for all these voices to have their own say without anyone else's being shut out.

We also trust that in working with U2 material in the pulpit we are honoring the fact that U2's art is itself consciously interactive, crafted so as to encourage personal appropriation and contributions. U2 clearly loves to break down the fourth wall and draw ordinary audience members in to interact with the spectacle; after all, they named their band after the concept. So these sermons, in one sense, are a particular subgroup of U2's long tradition of lay participation. The preachers in this book are like the aspiring guitarist invited to lead "People Get Ready," the surprise "Mysterious Ways" belly dancer pulled up from the audience, the real Chilean mothers who took the microphone to name their "disappeared" sons on live TV during the Santiago Popmart concert.

But the reverse is true as well: we who preach also mount a spectacle and offer a way of seeing the world. Corporate Christian worship enacts a whole universe of meaning of which the sermon is a key part. So we, in turn, are pulling pieces of popular culture—something ordinary from the world of the hearer—up onstage into our show, into the universe of Gospel truth, and inviting them to dance with us for a few minutes. And in doing so, we are making a very similar statement to the one U2 makes: This world being evoked up front is not closed to you; you can recognize yourself here; there is no difference between you and me; anyone can be part of this.

It is those encounters, when ordinary meets extraordinary and secular opens to sacred, which let us know in our bones that transformation is possible. We've tasted that transformation through the work of U2; we hope you taste it in these sermons.

october/
new year's day

*After this I looked, and there was a great
multitude that no one could count, from every
nation, from all tribes and peoples and
languages, standing before the throne and
the Lamb, robed in white, with palm branches
in their hands. They cried out in a loud voice,
"Salvation belongs to our God, who is seated
on the throne, and to the Lamb!"*

— Rev. 7:9–10

It's the wildest of dreams, to think that a time is coming
when all the divisions over which we've fought wars and
inflicted countless wrongs against each other will mean as
little to us as they do to God. A time when all the colors will
bleed into one and every tribe will gather in a peaceable kingdom ruled by one who acts as servant to all.

It's wilder than that to see how vivid that dream is among
some who are in the thick of the strife. Except that here the
dream is hope, and hope is by definition seeing things that in
the present are nowhere to be seen.

What gives the activist the courage to face tear gas and
police batons and the prisoner the strength to pray for her
torturers? What gives the addict the strength to set aside the

needle or the bottle for an hour and the person stuck in a bleak moment the courage to walk on? What, if not the hope that things will be different, if not the determination to see the dream of God's future more vividly than the realities of the present?

Desmond Tutu had a vision of the day he would vote in free elections in South Africa: "The sky looked blue and more beautiful. I saw the people in a new light. They were beautiful, they were transfigured. I too was transfigured. It was dreamlike. You were scared someone would rouse you and you would awake to the nightmare that was apartheid's harsh reality."[1] That dream sustained him until it became reality for a nation, and he was able to write those words about the experience of casting his first vote.

When the trees are stripped bare of what they hold for a season, they reveal what is permanent, the bones reaching to embrace a sky of clouded promise. Such a revelation is "apocalyptic"—literally, from the Greek, "removing the cover" of the times to expose the reality of the dream. The prisoner is the one who is free, the rich man poor, the lowest exalted. There is no map to this territory, no name for the roads there, only the dreamer's heart beating: Faith. Hope. Love. This is the day.

Sarah Dylan Breuer

1 Desmond Tutu, *No Future Without Forgiveness* (New York: Doubleday, 1999), 5–6.

There's a heaviness in the air. . .

Raewynne J. Whiteley

Song reference: "Beautiful Day"
Biblical reference: Genesis 9:8–17

A song by the Irish band U2 has been running through my mind these last few days. It captures some of what I'm feeling as I listen to the TV and the conversations around me, as I read the newspaper and the ancient words of the book of Genesis.

> See the world in green and blue
> See China right in front of you
> See the canyons broken by cloud
> See the tuna fleets clearing the sea out
> See the Bedouin fires at night
> See the oil fields at first light

It's a picture of the earth that we know so well from satellite images—deep blue and rich green, with patches of brown where the ground is less fertile, and caps of white. And away from the sun, dark shadows mark the continents, sprinkled with pinpricks of light. Yesterday afternoon I could see London and Delhi and Baghdad.

It is an incredibly beautiful picture, a picture which our ancestors could not have imagined, and yet, as we get closer, the extent of human impact can be seen too clearly: a row of oil wells flaming in Saudi Arabia, oil slicks in the Arabian Sea, and deforestation in the Amazon. All that beauty, and all that destruction, the essential ambiguity of life on earth—and that is just our natural world. Satellites can't begin to catalogue the human tragedies which surround us: poverty, disease, war. And more is yet to come.

There is a heaviness in the air, even as spring comes, a heaviness of waiting and uncertainty. In just over a week, we may well be at war, and I think none of us knows what that may mean. Some commentators have said that this will be a quick war, over in a matter of days thanks to the superior firepower of the United States. But others warn of a far more grim prospect, weeks lengthening into months, as ordinary people fight not for their leaders but for their homes and livelihoods and dignity.

And whether it is short or long, there will be deaths, deaths on both sides, the innocent and the guilty alongside one another, and as is the way of such things, the poor and the struggling will have the most to suffer, regardless of which side they are on: those who can't afford to heat their homes or drive to work because of upwardly spiraling oil prices, those who have gone to war because the military is the only way they could think of to get themselves a college education, those who had the misfortune to be born in that place and who have no chance to escape, those who have been conscripted to fight a war not of their own making.

There is a hopelessness about it all. Behind the rhetoric of our leaders and the pride in our fellow citizens lurks a hopelessness and a helplessness because there is so little we can do, as we sit in our living rooms and watch the world head into war.

How has it come to this? Not just the situation with Iraq, but the situation of our world. Weapons of mass destruction spoken of as casually as toy guns. Mothers filling their shopping carts with plastic and duct tape alongside diapers and Band-Aids and apple sauce. Shoppers arrested in shopping malls for wearing T-shirts with peace slogans. And underneath it all, the fear that somehow war in Iraq will escalate or that North Korea will take an opportunity while attention is elsewhere or that by government decision or terrorist action we will all be caught up in conflict of unimaginable proportions.

Some of us are too young to remember the 1950s "duck and cover" campaign, but even as we laugh at the innocence and futility of it, there was at least a sense that there was something you could do in the face of the atom bomb. I remember the threats of the 1970s, a time when many of us who were children at the time expected to die, sooner or later, as a result of nuclear attack. Children's fantasy fiction told stories of a return to savagery among those who might survive; we were given writing assignments on Armageddon.

Today, the fears are not so much around nuclear attack but around the far more ordinary things that can so easily be turned into weapons of war: airplanes, postal systems, drinking water, dirty bombs, smallpox. The list is endless. There is only so much we can do; mostly, we are helpless, and so we wait. And it seems to me that a big part of that helplessness, that fear, is that the world as we know it is under threat. Threat of breakdown, the breakdown of buildings, of infrastructure, of society as we know it.

And it is all too easy to imagine that God has abandoned us. Abandoned us not so much as individuals—we can still pray and worship and experience God at work among us—but abandoned us on the earthly scale. Sometimes, as we look at what is going on around us, it seems as if God has abandoned the human race, left us to our own devices, to the consequences of our own flawed decision making. Sometimes it seems as if there is no future for us at all.

But the image of the world of U2's song is not so hopeless.

See the world in green and blue
See China right in front of you
See the canyons broken by cloud
See the tuna fleets clearing the sea out
See the Bedouin fires at night
See the oil fields at first light
And see the bird with a leaf in her mouth
After the flood all the colors came out

In the middle of hopelessness, in the middle of our ambiguous and fractured world, there is a story, a story of another time when the world was bent on destroying itself. A story from the very foundations of our faith. The story of Noah.

You may remember the story. The world has got itself into so much of a mess that God decides to begin again. God decides to destroy everything except a family and some animals—enough to repopulate the land.

It's a difficult story. We don't like to think of a God who would go and destroy everything just because the human race had made a mess of it. We don't like to think of it because we know that we are constantly messing up, and the last thing we want is to be put in the hands of a God who just might decide to abandon us and begin all over again. It's a difficult story, because it belongs to a way of looking at the world which is very different from ours.

But if we try to step into the shoes, just for a moment, of the people who first told the story, then it is very different indeed. They had no satellite views of the earth, no pictures from far off of a beautiful green and blue globe. All they had was what they could see, and what they could see was frightening. Things happened without warning. Storms and earthquakes, famine and plenty, all came without any real reason. One moment you were safe, and the next, dead.

And there were consequences to everything. Justice was simple. You hurt someone; they hurt you back, eye for eye, limb for limb, life for life. Your child or wife or servant made a mistake, and you punished them. Your very survival depended on it. If that was your world, the actions of God in this story seemed perfectly reasonable. Put an end to evil and begin again.

But the surprise comes in the last bit of the story. Noah and his family and all the animals have been cooped up in the ark, day after day, as the rain pours down. Until finally it stops, and they begin to see the tops of mountains. They send out a bird, and it returns with a branch in its beak, a leaf in its mouth. And they know that the cycle of life has begun again.

But that is not the end of the story. God speaks. God speaks—not words of condemnation but words of hope, of promise, of grace. And God gives a sign, a splash of color across the sky.

Never again will this happen. Never again will the earth be destroyed. Never again. The rainbow is a sign.

See the world in green and blue
See China right in front of you
See the canyons broken by cloud
See the tuna fleets clearing the sea out
See the Bedouin fires at night
See the oil fields at first light
And see the bird with a leaf in her mouth
After the flood all the colors came out

In the middle of our helplessness we wait for a sign from God; in the middle of our hopelessness, we wonder what sort of future we will have.

But the sign has come, a promise that never again will the earth be destroyed. A leaf in the mouth of a bird, a splash of color in the sky. Life will continue, even in the most difficult places. There is a robustness to our world, a robustness rooted in the very heart of God.

And no matter what happens in the days ahead, God's promise still stands, and we can have faith in a future of peace, peace which comes not from military force but from the very heart of God.

Trinity Episcopal "Old Swedes" Church
Swedesboro, NJ
9 March 2003, Lent 1, Year B

To See What You See:
On Liturgy & Learning & Life
Steven Garber

Song reference: "When I Look At The World"
Biblical reference: Psalm 123

One day last spring I was working at home. In point of fact, I was on the phone, talking to someone doing research on the meaning of religious faith in higher education. In the middle of the conversation my son Elliott and his roommate Seth Wispelwey walked in, on their way back to the University of Virginia after a spring break trip to New York City. It was a surprise; I hadn't expected them.

As I saw them, I smiled. Sometimes you have news for someone that you *know* is going to rock their world. Their eyes will grow huge, their jaws will drop, and a smile that comes from the deepest place will soon be ear-to-ear. Have you ever had news like that for someone?

And so, with significant delight and a pretense of innocence, I said to them, "Hey, do you have any interest in coming to a meeting with Bono this afternoon?" For two college students who love music, who care about ideas and what they mean for life, and who had made a pilgrimage earlier in the year to one of the first concerts of the Elevation Tour because they are big fans of the biggest band in the history of rock and roll, this was good news—close to gospel.

Well, a couple hours later we walked into the Capitol buildings, and there he was: Paul Hewson himself, Bono, chief musician of the band U2. But he wasn't there to sing "Where the Streets Have No Name," or even to draw attention to his artistry or himself. Not for a moment, not for a million moments. Instead he wanted to talk about Africa, in particular, why Christians should care about Africa.

The twenty-five or so in the room represented all different sectors of Washington life, all different kinds of vocations: the World Bank, the White House, the State Department, USAID, the Congress, World Vision, even the Council for Christian Colleges and Universities. There were politicians, journalists, medical researchers, economists, professors.

And Bono was remarkably humble, thanking us for taking the time to talk to him, with "flowers in my hair, and stars in my eyes." At least, he said, that is what we might assume about him. But then he went on to explain why his interest in Africa was something other than a passing fad, a celebrity cause—why in fact it grew out of his deepest commitments about the way the world is and ought to be, out of his love for and loyalty to Jesus and the gospel of the kingdom.

As he spoke, I looked around the room. I was in awe of the expertise: people at the very pinnacle of their own vocations, some of the best of the best at what they do. World-class but not worldly, sophisticated but not cynical, each and every one was a person who prays and works—day after day after day— to see the world the way that God does, and then chooses to so form his or her own hopes and dreams, vocations and occupations, in ways which are faithful to that vision.

They are people who "get it"—as in, I wonder why she doesn't "get it." Or, he "gets it," doesn't he? There is something about heart and mind together in that assessment. They are people who are more than smart, because they understand that it is possible to get all A's and still flunk life. In biblical imagery, they are people with ears that hear, and eyes that see. They are people who know that to know—in a deeply biblical sense—means to be responsible, and that to be responsible means to care. They are people who understand that deeply Christian discipleship is marked by learning to see the world the way that God does, to know the world the way that God does, to love the world the way that God does. Did you ever see the cartoon, set in a college classroom, where the professor fills up two whiteboards with mathematical calculations? You know, letters and numbers out the wazoo. It is a kind of math I left behind a long time ago, which is not to my credit! After the complex relationships between addition and subtraction, multiplication and division are set forth, and most of us find ourselves overwhelmed, not sure what to do with all that we have seen, there is a seemingly simple "equals" sign on the far side of the second board. And there is one word: Whatever.

Whatever. Whatever. Whatever. For many, that word captures our feelings as we look at the world, full of complex sadness and sorrow, multifaceted injustice and evil. Simply put, we don't know what to say or do, because we don't know what to make of what we see. I meet students all over the world who feel this way. They do care, they want to engage God's world, but when they touch it, when they see it and smell it, too often it crushes them, it overwhelms them in the complexity of its griefs.

Psalm 123 is a song born out of that anguish, out of that confusion. Brutality, arrogance, powerful people crushing powerless people, and no cheap answers to the political and economic and social brokenness. What to do? To whom do I look? The psalmist says, "I look to you, I look to you for help! As the eyes of slaves look to the hand of their master, so our eyes look to you, Lord our God—until you show us mercy."

To whom and to what do we look when the world presses in upon us, when incoherence and fragmentation seem all that is possible, if we are to be really honest? These heartaching words of the psalm are a lament, yes. But they are also a song of hard-won affection and respect. There is no final despair here. No deep-seated cynicism. These are words of trust. "Lord, my eyes are fixed on you, I offer my heart to you because I trust you to show mercy. Have mercy on us, O Lord, have mercy!"

One of the deep truths of the Bible is that we all, sons of Adam and daughters of Eve each one, see out of our hearts. It is no small thing that Calvin College sets forth in its motto, year by year, generation upon generation, this vision: to you, Lord, I give my heart, promptly and sincerely. These words represent the possibility of coherence, rather than incoherence—because we do see out of our hearts. These words represent the possibility of a life of integrity across the spectrum of our responsibilities as human beings, rather than the inevitability of a fragmented existence—because we do see out of our hearts. Am I just a rat in the cage (Billy Corgan and the Smashing Pumpkins)? Should we all just eat, drink, and be merry, for tomorrow we die (The Dave Matthews Band)? An education at Calvin is set amidst the questions and tensions of life in a fallen world, and if it is worth the time and money it will speak into those questions and tensions with sensitivity and responsibility. The words set on the seal of the college give us a window into the possibility that belief and behavior in every arena of life can find its coherence in Jesus as Lord; that the truest integrity is always and everywhere found in offering myself to God, promptly and sincerely; that we can weave together liturgy, learning, and life.

The word liturgy seems to belong in a space like this. We speak of a liturgy for worship, meaning an ordering of worship, a way of worship. But the word itself is richer, if I can say it that way. It has to do with the whole of life, everyday, ordinary life. It comes from a Latin word which means, simply, *service,* the work one does on behalf of the community.

It is a good word for times like this, when the community of Calvin College gathers to sing and pray, to hear the word of God together. But it is also a good word for what happens when we leave this building and go to the ones next door, where philosophical questions are probed, where languages are learned, where counseling is done, where money is counted, where faculty are hired, where students are admitted, and on and on and on. Have you ever wondered about the possibility of a liturgy of learning, a liturgy of life? About the integral character of a heart given promptly and sincerely to God, and therefore a graceful seamlessness between liturgy and learning and life?

Well, I do, all the time. In a sense it is the question of my life, and so I am always looking for people who live this way.

Bono is this kind of person. How else do we make sense of songs like "Gloria" and "Grace," how else do we understand the almost sacramental and amazingly skillful character of U2's music (a quality that makes them perhaps the most famous artists in the world today), and at the same time know that Bono has committed himself to Africa for the long haul, for a long obedience in the same direction? As a good friend of mine at the World Bank put it, after the meeting last spring, "You know, Bono is serious, isn't he?" Can Bono save the world? No, never. That was *Time* magazine's cover story and question the week of our meeting last spring. He will not save the world, but he can—in his own words—write songs that make the light a bit brighter, that tear a little corner off of the darkness.

Brian is this kind of person too. Born out of the soil of a community in northern New Jersey where worship, worldview, and way of life were equally honored, he came to Calvin College as a pre-med student and found here professors and peers who nourished that seamless character of faith. Years later he is a professor of medicine at the University of Virginia in Charlottesville. Brian is extremely competent and very passionate, but honestly humble too. I have never heard him say this, but those who know say about him: He knows more about AIDS in Africa than anyone else in America, maybe the world.

When the meeting was called for March 12, last spring, I called Brian and invited him to come. I knew that Bono's love for Africa, particularly the project he is calling DATA, would be of more than passing interest to Brian, given his own commitments and cares. And so he came. When he got there, he was surprised to see his son, Seth, my son's roommate and friend. Yes, Seth Wispelwey is the son of Brian Wispelwey.

Twenty-five years after coming to Calvin College, Brian is still offering his heart promptly and sincerely to God, in his worship, his worldview, and his way of life. By the grace of God, Brian "gets it." He understands that a Calvin degree has to mean something, it has to have consequence for the world, that his learning and his life are rooted in the reality that we are called to see the world as God does, to know it in its glories and shames, and to still care for it—Brian understands that.

And so, in imitation of Christ, day after day Brian takes up his scientific skill to serve the aches and pains of the world. In imitation of Christ, he sees places and people who need his gifts, his passions, and his commitments, and takes up the towel of medical research, giving his service to the university and to the world.

So I try to be like you
Try to feel it like you do . . .
I can't wait any longer
I can't wait 'til I'm stronger
Can't wait any longer
To see what you see
When I look at the world

It is in the imitation of Christ that each of us finds our true vocation—butcher, baker, candlestick maker. Or musician and medical school professor. Simply said, Jesus came to serve, not to be served. And the text in John 13 is perhaps the clearest window we have into the meaning of that service, as in it we have the incarnation of God's response to the lament of Psalm 123. "Show us your mercy"—and God did, in the flesh.

The passage makes an important point for those of us here at Calvin, working our way through a curriculum shaped by words like creation, fall, and redemption. John writes that it was because Jesus was situated in the grand story of God's work in the world—himself embodying the history of redemption from creation to consummation—knowing where he had come from and where he was going, that he had eyes to see, that he could make sense of the responsibility before him, and therefore gave himself in service to meet the need of his brothers, washing their feet, their dirty, dusty feet. Because Jesus knew, he cared—a morally meaningful response was built into the very act of knowing.

Remembering this is important for all of us, perhaps especially for those who wonder whether Calvin College dreamed all this up, this creation, fall, and redemption stuff! The good news is that it is history, it is the way the world really is. And these ideas have legs. They are the contours for human life under the sun. They were for Jesus, they are for Bono and Brian, and they will be for us—taking up towels as we labor together as an academic community in class and out, living as citizens in our time and place, and praising and praying and pondering the meaning of God's work in history for our lives and for the whole of life.

Calvin College Chapel
9 October 2002

Not Afraid to Die, Not Afraid to Live

Henry VanderSpek

Song reference: "Kite"
Biblical reference: Isaiah 25:8

There it was. Like the Big Ben of the Internet looming large before me on a dark and stormy night. What would it tell me? When would the fateful hour be? I was feeling fit that day, so I chose "optimistic." I entered a few pieces of personal information like any other website—easier than my last online book order actually—and then clicked the wide blood-red button at the bottom of the page.

In a split second it was there. A small JavaScript box with a tombstone marked "R.I.P." and a skull popped up before me. "Your personal day of death is . . . Tuesday September 26, 2056." I had about 1.6 billion seconds to live! Clock gears wheeled around as the seconds rapidly counted down before my eyes. It was jarring. Only 53 years left—in "optimistic" mode as well! What if I had chosen normal, sadistic, or even pessimistic mode?! And I will die on a Tuesday! Shallow thoughts went through my head, like "Will there still be half-price Tuesdays at the local cinema then? Maybe I'll even be in the cinema when it happens. Maybe afterwards? Maybe I can change what happens—stop it somehow like that *Back to the Future* movie?" My mind raced.

Of course I should have prepared myself for this new insight. The words of greeting on the website were clear enough:

> Welcome to the Death Clock, the Internet's friendly reminder that life is slipping away . . . second by second. Like the hourglass of the Net, the Death Clock will remind you just how short life is.

Death. It is inevitable. The book of Ecclesiastes states that death "is the destiny" of every person (Eccl. 7:2). The Psalms say that our days pass "like grass" and then are no more (Ps. 103:15). It's an upsetting concept, yet somehow popular. Deathclock.com has predicted the day and hour of death for millions. People pour out their spite and their admiration for the site in posted comments. Death is life's final marker, and its arrival time is always unknown. The finish line to life's race can come at any time for each of us. As such, it can become an ever-present fear.

As a longtime fan of U2, I have come to admire their courage in tackling some difficult subjects. Their music passionately explores the core of life's meaning. Songs like "With or Without You" or "I Still Haven't Found What I'm Looking For" exemplify a longing for a deeper level of living and relating. It is no surprise then that themes of life, and even death, would also thread their way through U2's songs.

It is also interesting that U2 enters the world of popular music—a world well-defined by the trio of "sex, drugs & rock 'n' roll"—dealing with such completely opposite matters. Going against the grain of shallow pop culture, their music rings with the reality of a wider embrace of life.

While U2's first album, Boy, dealt with the awkward transition from youth to the fuller life of adulthood, later albums soon began to deal with death. Here are just a few songs that trace this theme: "Sunday Bloody Sunday" marks the sad reality of Ireland's bloody history. "Pride (In The Name Of Love)" is about living unafraid of dying for love, and was most notably focused on Martin Luther King and his death. "Exit" is a song about suicide that Bono once said gave him chills to sing. "Where the Streets Have No Name" is arguably about heaven and the afterlife. "Until the End of the World" has Judas, the betrayer of Jesus, rising from the dead at the end of time to share his thoughts. As the years have gone on, U2 has been reflecting more and more on what death is all about. *All That You Can't Leave Behind,* some twenty years after their first album, finds the band stepping into a more mature phase of life. Perhaps it is the death of fellow rock stars, the ongoing troubles in Ireland, the band members all passing the milestone age of forty years, or the combination of all of these, but U2 recognizes mortality in a deeper way in this album. The reality of death casts its shadow on many of the songs—the title even plays with it—but somehow the music manages to face this reality in a way that is not depressing.

"Stuck In A Moment" opens with a line that is reminiscent of words from Martin Luther King's great speech the day before he was assassinated: "I am not afraid of anything in this world." Bono has acknowledged that this song was influenced by the suicide of Michael Hutchence, the lead singer of INXS. "In A Little While" deals with the moments of passing from this life into what lies beyond. It is said that Joey Ramone, from the early punk band The Ramones, took comfort in this song before he died.

But the place that U2 comes full face with death is in "Kite." During the Elevation Tour, Bono's father was critically ill and eventually passed away. "Kite" is the song Bono dedicated to him during his illness and after his death. Its words are particularly poignant:

> I'm not afraid to die
> I'm not afraid to live
> And when I'm flat on my back
> I hope to feel like I did

It is an honest song about being prepared and ready for one's own passing—a moment that can come at any time. I find it fascinating that in the middle of this song Bono sings very powerfully:

> I'm a man, I'm not a child
> A man who sees
> The shadow behind your eyes

He is echoing here similar words found—also in the middle—of one of the most famous passages on love ever written in the Bible or anywhere else:

When I was a child,
I spoke like a child,
I thought like a child,
I reasoned like a child;
When I became an adult,
I put an end to childish ways. (1 Cor. 13:11)

It seems that U2 has made the link that somehow coming into maturity involves facing the reality of death and acknowledging it. Author Robert Bly concurs. In his book *The Sibling Society*, he talks about how Western culture supports an environment where people are not encouraged to "graduate" to maturity, but rather can stay as immature adolescents throughout their lives. From plastic surgery and botox injections to the youth-obsessed media, examples of an immature culture are rampant.

It may be a bit of pop-psychology, but it is commonly recognized by counselors that the best way to deal with the pain of loss or trauma is to face up to it and go "through the wound"—feeling the pain and grieving it. Only then can one come to a place of true healing. We can never go forward unless we do so; otherwise we will be held back in an unhealthy pattern of denial and avoidance. Western culture as a whole is caught in this pattern when it comes to death.

Death as a reality is never a welcome fact in any culture, but particularly so in the West. It is "too heavy," it seems. Avoidance and denial are more ready forms of managing the fact that death exists and will one day touch even ourselves. Grief is tucked well away into the contained spaces of funeral homes. Bodies are handled by professionals with chemical preservatives to make them look as lifelike as possible.

Contrast this with a Middle Eastern funeral, where a loved one's body is prepared for death by family members. Some psychologists have suggested that this act is helpful for the grieving process as it helps make real the fact of death. A fact which we quite naturally want to avoid. In the Middle East a procession, often on foot, to the local cemetery makes personal grief much more public and visible to the larger community. While the slow sleek movements of a hearse leading a train of cars can be an emotional sight, it does not expose the pain and reality of the grieving in quite the same way. In my work with refugees, I have been fortunate to share meals and stories with people from many parts of the world. It has struck me as significant that in cultures in which death is more visible, or just more accepted as part of life, people seem to have an equally strong ability to celebrate. I find that there is often an element of denial in Western partying—a fleeing from reality through alcohol or drugs—instead of a wide embrace of all that reality has to offer. If that is the problem, that we are living a lie in our immature lives, then the maybe the antidote is a visit to Deathclock.com! Maybe seeing how many seconds we have left might help us to become mature adults who can celebrate with soul!

Perhaps part of the problem is that Western culture has lost the thread of reasoning and motivation to contemplate death. "Why bother with such a depressing task? Leave it to medieval monks to keep a skull on their desk for meditating on life's brevity! I've got things to do, places to go. Life is too short to walk around moping and being depressed. I need to make my mark in life."

It is interesting that "Kite" asks the question of life, "Did I waste it?" What allows one to really make a mark in this world? Those obsessed by beauty and youth are rarely remembered for their life's work. Only those who are freed from the fear of death—often hidden in an obsession with beauty, youth, wealth, or power—can really go on to accomplish great things. Mother Teresa and Martin Luther King will be remembered years after the most fashionable stars of their day. It is an ironic paradox that only once we get over our fear of death can we then begin to produce something significant and memorable.

What then can solve this dilemma? What can give any of us the courage to face up to the daunting and terrifying horror of death? How can we face it in the light of U2's music?

The Bible relates to this struggle with death and is replete with commentary on its significance. The apostle Paul calls death "the last enemy to be destroyed" (1 Cor. 15:26). Death is indeed a mighty foe to face up to.

But the Bible also holds out an answer. The answer is not an idea but a person—the person of Jesus. Jesus faced the challenge of death, carrying the weight of the world's pride and vanity—more commonly referred to by Christians as sin—and died on the cross. According to Scripture, the price of our vanity and pride is death, but "the free gift of God is eternal life in Christ Jesus" (Rom. 6:23). Jesus paid the price for our sin—dying for us—liberating us to live in a new and truly free way.

Paul reflects on this new reality by saying that "Death has been swallowed up in victory" (1 Cor. 15:54); that is, death was destroyed by Jesus' dying and rising again. In confidence he exclaims, "Where, O death, is your victory? Where, O death, is your sting?" (1 Cor. 15:55). The prophet Isaiah's words that God will "swallow up death forever" (Isa. 25:8) are fulfilled in what Jesus did. The truly tough work of looking death in the eye was done by Jesus. We just need to stand beside him, like a bullied child beside a strong parent. With Jesus beside us we can face death, because he has already faced it—and won.

And the words of "I Still Haven't Found What I'm Looking For" are a prayerful acknowledgment of this reality:

> You broke the bonds
> You loosed the chains
> Carried the cross and my shame
> And my shame,
> you know I believe it.

We are meant to grow toward full maturity. Like those powerful words Bono sang in "Kite," we are to become adults, not stay as children. A key step in this journey is facing the reality of death, the reality of our own sin and pride, and recognizing our need for help to do so. The one who conquered sin and death for us is the one we can turn to.

And God speaks words of comfort to those who trust in him:

> But now thus says the Lord,
> He who created you, O Jacob,
> he who formed you, O Israel:
> Do not fear, for I have redeemed you;
> I have called you by name, you are mine.

When you pass through the waters, I will be with you;
and through the rivers, they shall not overwhelm you.
(Isa. 43:1–2)

The God who breathed life into us knows the hour of our
death and will be with us when we pass to the other side. We
need not be afraid, only learn to walk in trust. This same
source of confidence is our source of life and passion for living. Whether Deathclock.com tells you you have thirty years
or thirty days left to live, a life lived knowing that death has
been conquered will not be wasted but will indeed be, as U2
sings, "fragrant, rooftop to the basement."

Fall 2002

Temples of an Incarnate God

David Friedrich

Song reference: "The Playboy Mansion"
Biblical references: 2 Samuel 7:4, 8–16; Luke 1:26–38

That there is a force of love and logic behind the universe is overwhelming to start with, if you believe it. . . . But the idea that that same love and logic would choose to describe itself as a baby born in shit, straw and poverty, is genius. And [it] brings me to my knees, literally."[2] These were the words of Bono as he made his way through the American Midwest raising awareness of both the epidemic of AIDS in Africa and the crushing third world debt. A voice crying in the wilderness not unlike that of John the Baptist we've been hearing throughout the Advent season.

In the readings for today, two very interesting scenes address the way in which God chose to enter creation. The Hebrew Scripture from 2 Samuel is a message from God being given to the prophet Nathan. The scene leading up to this word from the Lord is a conversation between King David and Nathan. David is feeling guilty because he is living in a nice "house of cedar" while the Ark of the Covenant (the symbol of God's presence) is being housed in a tent. At first,

2 Cathleen Falsani, "Bono Issues Blunt Message for Christians," *Chicago Sun-Times*, 3 December 2002.

Nathan encourages David to build the Temple, but God has something else in mind. God's message to David is "You will not be the one to build a Temple, but what I will do is give you a dynasty and your kingdom will go on forever." The royal line begun with David was not put in place primarily to preside over housing God's presence in a physical place. Instead, it was to be a vehicle for the presence of God to enter the world in a truly radical way—the womb of a young woman in a nowhere town.

And so we go to the second scene, in the gospel of Luke. The angel Gabriel appears to Mary, a young woman in Nazareth minding her own business, and calls her to be the vehicle for the presence of God, God with us, Emmanuel. Not surprisingly, she experiences a series of reactions:

She is perplexed: I should say so! And she hasn't even heard the whole message!

She ponders: thoughtful, even critical, but open.

She questions: obviously!

She answers: "Let it be with me according to your will."

God called a young woman in the middle of nowhere to be a fitting temple to bring into the world God in human form. She answered with a resounding "Yes!" God continues to call people to be vehicles, temples, of the incarnation. What is our answer as individuals and as a community?

U2 paints an intriguing picture of a different sort of vehicle, a worldly temple, by imagining a mansion.

If coke is a mystery
michael jackson history
if beauty is truth
and surgery the fountain of youth
what am I to do
have I got the gifts to get me through
the gates of that mansion

This mansion is one of falsities. The criterion for getting in revolves around superficiality and triviality. One has to have the right perspective and the right looks to be worthy. The temple of the body only has to look good on the outside.

If o.j. is more than a drink
and a big mac bigger than you think
if perfume is an obsession
and talk shows . . . confession
what have we got to lose
another push and maybe we'll be through
the gates of that mansion

What kind of mansion is this? What kind of temple is being alluded to? If all it takes to enter is to understand burgers and perfume, maybe it's easier than we thought! How do we respond to a world where mysteries are the ingredients of soft drinks, where people use daytime talk shows to air their deepest secrets and the most intimate moments of their lives for the amusement of others? Something has got to give!

Throughout Advent we focus on the return of Christ to set right the wrongs of the world. We need that same love and logic that was born so humbly ages ago to return again into the world in a powerful way. "Love, come on down!" We need the power of Christ's return to break the perversion of the world and its trivializing of the human experience. Why are we more concerned with the latest TV reality show when there are people in the world longing only for a meal or someone to love them? Why are these concocted situations so compelling and addicting when the reality of starvation, third world debt, and tragedy of war often are so far from our minds?

There has got to be a better way to go, something better we can invest in to become fitting temples of an incarnate God and not hollow constructions of a society obsessed with itself. As we wait for the anticipated return of Christ, there is much to be done. Jesus Christ is active in the world today. He is present in the people we meet daily. He is present in those we love and those we hate. He is naked and in prison, he is hungry and thirsty. We are called to be Christ to others and serve Christ in them, bringing about God's Rule of justice and peace on the earth.

It is a daunting task, one that can often be thankless and difficult. But it is one we are called to nevertheless. We are called to be vehicles of God's presence in the world changing it with a radical new message of hope. This message is grounded in the very nature of who we understand God to be, a God who is willing to enter into the brokenness and poverty of our world and of our hearts in order to redeem it all.

The world can look sometimes awfully bleak, and the promise of the return of Christ may be hard to hold on to. The call of God to work for justice in the world may seem too difficult. These words of U2 may resonate more than the resounding "Yes" of Mary's answer.

don't know if I can wait that long
till the colors come flashing
and the lights go on
then will there be no time of sorrow
then will there be no time for shame
though I can't say why
I know I've got to believe

A glorious day will come when the colors will flash, the lights will go on and all sorrow and shame will be swallowed up by the radiance of Christ's return, setting the world right again. But we are not on our own until that day. Like Mary, we are all being invited by God to be a part of the continuing presence and work of God in the world. We are invited to bear God into the world by the way we live and witness to our faith in Jesus Christ, bringing light into a world that often seems incredibly dark. We may go through similar reactions to those of Mary when we try to comprehend the things we feel God calling us to do. It may not always make sense or be easy, but even when it is hard to rationalize, it's okay to throw our hands up and cry, "Though I can't say why, I know I've got to believe!"

God is present with us today. God is present in the people around us, in the bread we break at communion, and most importantly, God will be present within each one of us if we are willing to make the room. Is there room?

Trinity Episcopal Church
Topsfield, MA
22 December 2002
Fourth Sunday of Advent

until the end of the world

dost thou betray me with a kiss?
Canst thou find hell about my lips? and miss
Of life, just at the gates of life and bliss?

— George Herbert, "The Sacrifice"[1]

The kiss betrayed me.

For months, I'd been traveling with him. I listened to him, comforted him, prayed with him, stood by him, shared my vision of how the world could be and how little and how much it would take to see things set right. I thought he understood, or was beginning to understand. "Do what you must," I'd said to him, knowing that it would cost, but that either of us would give our life's blood to see God's kingdom come on earth as it is in heaven. This was the object of our prayers together each day, and of our silent prayers each night as we drifted to sleep beside the crackle of the fire and the steady sound of the other's breathing. "Do what you must," I'd said, and I thought that he was steeling himself to act.

• • •

As the time drew near, I told myself that I acted for the sake of a kingdom worth more than my life or his. I talked about resurrection as if that would cancel the cost. I talked about love, and told myself I acted in love for him and for the world we wanted to save from itself and from our enemies. And when, in the garden, he took my hand and turned the tables, I told myself that he finally understood what I had been trying to teach him. "Do what you must," he said.

The kiss betrayed me.

In the moment I kissed him, my lies crumbled like the shell of a log burned to ash. He didn't take up the sword, as I thought he would. He didn't attack the soldiers and lead us to Jerusalem to destroy our enemies there. And suddenly it was all clear, stripped naked like the young man who had traveled with us and was now fleeing the soldiers. I had believed the lie that God's rule could be purchased with violence. The lie that the big idea was bigger than our lives. The lie that I knew what love is, and the biggest lie of all—that it was my love of God that overrode my love for him. All dust.

• • •

We cheer the martyrs and then we kill them for the same reason. We think we are on the side of the angels, and we grow impatient for God to lead the charge. We think we destroy life to save it, that we kill out of love for something bigger. We think that we win, that God wins, by striking our enemies. But in the kiss, in one moment of real contact, we are shown to be as empty as we are.

It is they, the ones who take pride only in self-giving love, who have more than our bankrupt imagination can envision. We can't buy or sell what they've got, and in the moment of the kiss, we finally can't deny it. The world of darkness and violence, of injustice and hatred, has ended, is ending, will end. The world they proclaim can't be stopped with the sword, the might of institutions, or the betrayal of a brother. The universe arcs toward the justice for which it aches, and the whole world—martyrs and traitors, soldiers and healers, lovers and lawyers—will one day echo the song of the angels: Holy, holy, holy is the God who is Love, who is now, who is then, who is ever. Amen.

Sarah Dylan Breuer

---

1 George Herbert, *The Complete English Poems,* ed. John Torbin (New York: Penguin Books, 1991), 24–25.

The Psalms, the Blues, and the Telling of Truth

Jamie Howison

Song reference: "40"
Biblical reference: Psalm 40

When I was in my twenties, I realized that every song I wrote was about me. I swore I wouldn't write another song until I wrote about something else; I didn't write a thing for ten years! When I started again, it was because I had started writing from the Psalms.
— Steve Bell[2]

The Psalms thus propose to speak about human experience in an honest, freeing way. This is in contrast to much of human speech and conduct, which is in fact a cover-up.
— Walter Brueggemann[3]

---

2   From an unpublished interview, October 2002.
3   Walter Brueggemann, *Praying the Psalms* (Winona, MN: Saint Mary's Press, 1993), 17.

That's what a lot of the psalms feel like to me, the blues. Man shouting at God—"My God, my God, why hast thou forsaken me? Why art thou so far from helping me?"

— Bono [4]

Steve Bell, Walter Brueggemann, and Bono: What links this singer/songwriter, Old Testament scholar and rock icon is the place of the Psalms in keeping their imaginations open and their lives in Christ authentic. This collection of ancient hymns is our "mother tongue," our first language of authentic discourse with and about God. They are "faith in the raw," or at least they are once we peel from them the layers of religiosity and numbness with which they have been laden. Set them free and read them again, and, in the words of Eugene Peterson, you find that "The Psalms in Hebrew are earthy and rough. They are not genteel. They are not the prayers of nice people, couched in cultured language." [5]

They are, by turns, as earthy as the crying tones of country music, as angry as punk, as anthemic as stadium rock, as comforting as a lullaby, as soulful and raw as the blues. Above all, as soulful and raw as the blues. "The Psalter may be a font of gospel music," writes Bono, "but for me it's in his despair that the psalmist really reveals the nature of his special relationship with God. Honesty, even to the point of anger." [6]

"Honesty, even to the point of anger." We are not much good at that kind of honesty in the church, and that is more than a bit of a deep irony. In the church, as in the wider society in which we live, there is a great deal of anger. But it does not seem to be an anger born of honesty so much as one born of frustration, despair, and an unwillingness (or inability?) to speak truthfully.

Brueggemann provides a helpful framework for describing what is going on here. He sets out a description of the life of faith, but I suspect it is something of a script for life in the human family generally. He writes:

---

4   Bono, "Introduction," *Selections from the Book of Psalms* (New York: Grove Press, 1999), viii.
5   Eugene H. Peterson, "Introduction to the Psalms," *The Message* (Colorado Springs: NavPress, 1995).
6   Bono, "Introduction," viii.

> I suggest, in a simple schematic fashion, that our life of
> faith consists in moving with God in terms of
>   a. being securely *oriented,*
>   b. being painfully *disoriented,* and
>   c. being surprisingly *reoriented.*[7]

Secure orientation, painful disorientation, surprising
reorientation; it is a movement that we see played out again
and again, both in our own lives and in the great human
drama. Perhaps there is not always and everywhere a secure
beginning, and clearly the experience of being "surprisingly
reoriented" is not universal. For many people, the best they
can hope is that they might learn to live with the pain or, perhaps, be sold something that could narcotize them into a
proverbially *false* sense of security. Nevertheless, the people of
God must live at least in openness to the surprisingness characteristic of our God.

Brueggemann argues that what the psalms do is to speak
into all of the phases of this cycle; that they "present 'all sorts
and conditions of men' and women addressed to the Holy
God."[8] And while there are clear examples that speak from
the perspective of secure orientation (Psalms 1, 14, 119, and
145, for example), more of the psalms are written out of experiences of dislocation and relocation. It is because they are
written *from* such experiences that they are able to speak back
into them. They speak into the disorientation "in an honest,
freeing way," writes Brueggemann, "in contrast to much of
human speech and conduct, which is in fact a cover-up."[9]

And so, the blues. "David was the first blues singer," writes
Bono. A man of faith who "believed it enough to get angry
when it looked like [God] wasn't coming through."[10] Never
mind the critical arguments about the Davidic authorship
(or non-authorship, as the arguments generally run): David is
to the Psalms what Elvis is to rock and roll, as Bono asserts
in his fine introduction to the Grove Press edition of the
Psalms. On the question of David's authorship, he writes,

---

7 Brueggemann, *Praying the Psalms,* 14.
8 Ibid., 15.
9 Ibid., 17.
10 Bono, in John Waters, *Race of Angels,* quoted in Steve Stockman,
Walk On (Relevant Books, 2001), 145.

"Who cares? I didn't buy Leiber and Stoller . . . they were just his songwriters . . . I bought Elvis."[11] David as Elvis, David as Robert Johnson, John Lee Hooker, Van Morrison, Leadbelly. David as the one *just* real enough to say something this raw:

> My God, my God, why have you forsaken me? (22:1)
> Indeed, I was born guilty,
> a sinner when my mother conceived me. (51:5)
> O God, why do you cast us off forever? (74:1)

The blues. Laments, the scholarly literature tends to call them. And they have an even darker cousin that goes beyond mere blues into stark anger and loathing. These are the psalms of vengeance, and they embody a kind of speech not to be shared in polite circles:

> Happy shall they be who take your little ones
> and dash them against the rock. (137:9)
> The righteous will rejoice when they see
> vengeance done;
> they will bathe their feet in the blood of the
> wicked. (58:10)

Who says such things? Who imagines delight in taking a footbath in the blood of even the worst of your enemies? Who thinks it even imaginable to smash a baby's head against the rocks? No, no, Christians must not think, pray, hope for such things—or so we have taught ourselves. We have so convinced ourselves that ours must be a polite and politically correct faith that we have squeezed these vengeance psalms, along with most of the tougher laments, to the edges of our lectionary. Taken together, these psalms make up more than a third of the Psalter, yet we use them sparingly. The truly vengeful psalms virtually never appear in Sunday worship, and the darker of the laments are largely reserved (often with select verses edited out) for Lent and Holy Week. Praise and worship is our primary corporate language, but we are rendered mute by this limited vocabulary. "Such worship," says Brueggemann, "is destructive because it requires persons to

---

11 Bono, "Introduction," xiii.

engage in enormous denial and pretense about how life really is."[12] We will be disoriented—that is our reality—and without a language to name it, we will not stand much of a chance of being ready to receive liberating reorientation. The blues again, but this time with the buzz-saw edge of punk, or the truth-telling wail of that particular strain of rock music that rarely cracks the top forty. Bruce Cockburn's rage against the attacks on the inhabitants of refugee camps in "If I Had a Rocket Launcher." Steve Bell's "Somebody's Gotta Pay," written to vent his anger over the sexual exploitation of his teenaged foster daughter. Bono snarling the lines of "Bullet the Blue Sky," voicing his disgust over American foreign policy in El Salvador. These guys are recalling us to something we have tended to forget: God wants it all, right down to the ugliest, nastiest, most poisonous of our reactions to disorientation.

Then (and really only then) there is this promise of reorientation. Surprising, grace-full reorientation. Sometimes it might be tough to say whether a particular psalm is written out of a stable orientation or a surprising reorientation; it might be possible for a psalm to speak to both. I suspect, though, that this much at least holds true: the psalms that have about them both a sense of consolation and a resilient yet ultimately unresolved hopefulness—these are the ones birthed in reorientation. They have resolution and reorientation, but there is also a measured maturity that keeps saying, "I'm not done with this road yet." It is not a distrust of God, but rather a healthy respect for the yet unseen contours of the road ahead. It is the blues again, just not of the downtrodden, howling sort. It is U2's remarkable song "40," the final song from 1983's *War* album. Written to close that potent and political album with something akin to prayer, "40" fuses the opening verses of Psalm 40 with a hybrid refrain borrowed from Psalm 6 and the prophet Isaiah.

---

12 Walter Brueggemann, quoted in Beth LaNeel Tanner, "How Long, O Lord! Will Your People Suffer in Silence Forever?" Stephen Breck Reid, ed. *Psalms and Practice* (Collegeville, MN: The Liturgical Press, 2001), 144.

I waited patiently for the Lord
He inclined and heard my cry
He brought me up out of the pit
Out of the miry clay

I will sing, sing a new song. . .
How long to sing this song?

You set my feet upon a rock
You made my footsteps firm
Many will see
Many will see and hear.

The lines from Psalm 40 reflect a thankful reorientation, while the refrain calls for a deeper, more final restoration, one not entirely available to us this side of the Kingdom of God. For many years, this was the closing song at U2 concerts. I was fortunate to see the band in Toronto's Maple Leaf Gardens in the mid-1980s, when this was the established pattern. As the band played "40," Bono engaged the audience in singing with him the refrain. As we sang, one by one the band members left the stage. Seventeen thousand voices accompanied by guitar, bass and drums; then by bass and drums; by drums alone; and finally we sang *a cappella* until the house lights came up and we knew the evening had drawn to its close. Smiling, strangely subdued and peaceful, we wandered out of the arena to make our various ways home. So peaceful, in fact, as to be almost surreal. Something about ending a concert by singing (together!) a refrain of hope and longing, set in a song of consolation and reorientation, sounded a deep chord.

Maybe that is what these psalms are finally about: The sounding of deep, resonant, and truthful chords. And they are ours. Our language, our emotions, our issues, our mother tongue. They kick with the loneliness of the blues, the heartache of country, the anger of punk, the beauty of the string quartet. And we need them all, to keep us honest and moving. "How long to sing this song?" Probably for as long as we have need of the sounding of deep chords. Really, then, for as long as we yet have breath to sing.

Diocese of Rupert's Land, Clergy Continuing Education
31 October 2002

Wake Up Dead Man:
Singing the Psalms of Lament

Brian J. Walsh

Song reference: "Wake Up Dead Man"
Biblical reference: Psalm 44

When was the last time you heard a lament psalm recited or performed in your church with all of the emotional power and pathos that those psalms embody? You know, one of those psalms that lay it all on the line before the throne of God and demand that the Holy One give a response? Not too recently, I'll wager. In fact, if your church follows the Common Lectionary, then whenever those psalms appear they are sanitized by simply omitting the most abrasive sections.

Why? Why do we tend to avoid the psalms of lament? Well, they just don't seem to match what most of us think to be appropriate piety. I mean, if you are going to speak to God, then you have to be polite, don't you? You know, language about God's goodness, his grace, his love, his faithfulness. And bringing to the divine attention not only God's failures, but also his faults—well that is theologically problematic and downright impolite. And certainly we must be polite to God, right? No, these psalms are too abrasive, they threaten to undermine our praise, they are dangerous and scary. Indeed, some of these psalms seem to be nothing less than an assault on the supremacy and transcendence of God. You can't do that sort of thing in church!

Now think for a moment: if we were to write such psalms of lament today and perform them in public, what would they sound like? What kind of language would they employ? It seems to me that they would likely sound like abrasive, in-your-face, mournful and angry rock and roll, blues, hip hop, grunge, and rap music. And maybe the kind of language they would use might be something like the opening lines of U2's song, "Wake Up Dead Man."

> Jesus, Jesus help me
> I'm alone in this world
> and a fucked up world it is too

What? You can't sing that in church! You can't use language like that when addressing the Son of God! Well, hold that objection for a minute and reflect with me on Psalm 44.

In light of our censoring of lament, our covering-up of impolite piety, it is an amazing thing that Psalm 44 is in the Bible. For some reason, Israel thinks that shouting at God to "wake up, stop sleeping and stop hiding your face" is not an act of impiety. And this is because biblical faith and biblical spirituality refuse to cover up and deny the painful realities of betrayal, suffering, failure, and confusion. Biblical faith refuses any escapist spirituality of prayerful politeness because the God with whom we are dealing is a covenantal God. And because he is a covenantal God, he is always in the fray of life with us. A faith characterized by covenant is uncompromisingly dialogical and even confrontational because this God, as covenant partner, is answerable to us.

All of this, of course, shakes a passive and docile spirituality to its core. We censure the psalms of lament because we want to silence the voice of pain. And we silence the voice of pain because it is too unruly and too dangerous in its undermining of the status quo. Lament says, "Damn it, I'm not going to put up with this shit anymore!" Lament says, "The powers of normalcy be damned, I insist upon things being different. I insist upon God keeping his promises and bringing healing and justice to my life and the life of the most vulnerable, and I am not going to shut up until he hears my cry and answers me!"

Psalm 44 is such a voice of lament, such a whistle-blowing voice that refuses the cover-up. The psalmist begins by outlining the radical discontinuity between the story of salvation that is the very foundation of the believing community's identity and their present experience. We know the story, Lord. We know the story of your mighty deeds—how you planted us and set us free from slavery, how you saved us from our enemies. And we are very clear that this narrative legitimates no self-justifying triumphalism on our part. No, it is not our military prowess that has given us a place in the land, it is your right hand and your light-bearing presence that has illuminated our path and given us this wonderful gift of a home in which to practice covenant. We know the story, Lord. This is our story, this is our song.

But there is a radical dissonance between this story, this memory, and our present reality. You see, Lord, the people you planted are now scattered and the people you set free have now been taken captive. There's something wrong here, Lord; the plot of the narrative has got stuck somewhere. You see, slavery and the life of exiled nomads were part of the past plot of this narrative, and surely they have no place in the story at *this* time.

Something has gone terribly wrong. How did this happen? How did our story get so disastrously inverted? How did slaves set free by a liberating God become slaves again? Who is responsible for this tragic twist of history? The psalmist does not mince words and does not draw back from making a profound, seemingly blasphemous judgment:

> *You* have rejected us and humiliated us.
> *You,* our shepherd king, have made us sheep for
> the slaughter.
> *You,* our exodus liberator, have sold us cheaply
> into slavery. (cf. Ps. 44:9–12)

And we could understand all of this, Lord, *if* we had broken covenant. Then it would all make sense. If we had walked the path of idolatry, trying to pull a fast one on you, O Lord, then our malaise would be of our own making. But—and this is the clincher for the psalmist's complaint—we have been faithful! We have not broken covenant. And if *we* didn't break trust, then there is only one explanation for what is going on here. *You,* Lord, broke trust!

So here's the question, God: Where are you? Why are you hiding? Why do you forget our affliction and oppression? Don't you know that remembering is at the heart of our covenantal life with you? We haven't forgotten! Have you? Take a look, God; we're groveling in the dirt. So rise up! Don't leave us here! Remember who you are—the God of steadfast love! So, for the sake of that love, for the sake of that covenantal faithfulness, redeem us, liberate us again from our oppression.

> Rouse yourself! Why do you sleep, O Lord?
> Awake, do not cast us off forever!
> Why do you hide your face?
>
> Rise up, come to our help. (Ps. 44:23–24,26)

Now let's come back to U2's song, "Wake Up Dead Man." Notice any parallels here? It sounds like this song is the band's late-twentieth-century take on this ancient psalm. Taking a cue from the psalmist's bold "Rouse yourself! Why do you sleep, O Lord? Awake!", the song's refrain is "Wake up, wake up dead man."

But U2's "Wake Up Dead Man" is no more abrasive a lament than is the psalm. Indeed, the parallels are remarkable. The singer is alone in the world, the community of the psalmist has been abandoned by its God. The psalmist rehearses the narrative of redemption, the song invites Jesus to

> tell me, tell me the story
> the one about eternity
> and the way it's all gonna be

Tell me again that hope-engendering story that seems now to have reached a dead end.

And while the psalmist tells God the story as a reminder and as a basis for the lament, concluding with calling God back to his steadfast love, the song transposes the "*Shema* Israel" ("Listen Israel") into a "*Shema* Jesus," inviting Jesus to listen. If Jesus will only hear again his own words, then he will be able to hear *through* and *over* the cacophony of our post-modern confusion with its top forty trash, all-pervasive technology, urban oppressiveness, and militarism. Then maybe Jesus will be able to listen *to* the reed of the saxophone playing out its lament, and listen *as* hope and peace try to rhyme. Listening to your own words, Jesus, will give you discernment between the deafening cacophony of our times and the real voices of lament and hope.

The opening language of living in a "fucked up world" notwithstanding, U2's psalm of lament is actually *less* abrasive than the biblical psalm. You see, the song wonders whether Jesus is able to help. "Maybe your hands aren't free," muses the lyric; maybe you were busy when the calamity hit, "working on something new." The psalmist, however, is not so gentle. He refuses to let God off the hook precisely because he places the responsibility for this time of troubles squarely in God's court:

> you rejected us
> you humiliated us
> you made us turn back
> you made us like sheep for slaughter
> you sold us for a trifle
> you made us a taunt for our neighbors
> you made us a laughing stock
> you have broken us

Let's be clear. It is more risky to recite Psalm 44 in church than to sing "Wake Up Dead Man."

But both songs end up in the same place. Both the psalmist and U2 have the audacity to raise a voice of lament that calls upon our divine covenant partner to wake up. But in both instances, it is a wake-up call sung from a stance not of disbelief, but of faith. The psalmist confesses, "You are my King and my God," and U2 is still sure that Jesus is "looking out for us." The problem is that this kingship, this "looking out," is taking strange and unacceptable turns. To call this God to wake up, then, is an expression of profound faith. Adopting neither a history-stifling, covering-up conservative docility, nor a numbed-out, paralyzed cynicism, both the psalm and the song are willing to take the risk of prayer. By demanding that God wake up to their respective tragedies, they are taking the risk that God just might do that. By uttering their abrasive prayers, they are giving voice to a faith that says that this God can handle being spoken to in such terms and that such cries of pain are precisely what motivates this God to redemptive action.

Do we have the honesty, courage, and audacity to give full voice to such laments in our own time? And do we give space for such complaints, such voices of pain, confusion and disappointment in the midst of our communal life at prayer?

"Redeem us for the sake of your steadfast love," ends the psalm. "Your Father, he made the world in seven / He's in charge of heaven / will you put a word in for me," confesses the song. These laments are rooted in faith—faith in a Creator God who, contrary to appearances, is sovereign over history, and who is still characterized by steadfast love. This steadfast love of God, this covenant-keeping fidelity, is our final court of appeal. It authorizes our lament, grounds our trust, and engenders our hope.

Student conferences in Canada

Deliverance Where the Streets Have No Name

Stephen Butler Murray

Song reference: "Where the Streets Have No Name"
Biblical reference: Psalm 40:1–5,11–13,16–17

It is the constantly surprising nature of churches to endure through difficult times that weds me to the strange and wonderful roles of preacher and pastor. It is what makes me think that on days when we are dealing with tragedies, it is important to get into the pulpit. It is important to remember that church goes on despite our sadness. In fact, it is *essential* that church goes on, because it is in worship, in fellowship, in song, in prayer that we find ourselves renewed, restored, our very lives affirmed. We do what we do in church not to escape the pain that the world sometimes brings to bear upon us, but to embrace the totality and complexity of all that life yields. Sometimes we hurt. And sometimes we cry. Sometimes we laugh. And sometimes we rejoice. All of it, all the vagaries of life, we go through here. Never alone. Always with each other. Always with God.

As a community that lives on the threshold of Manhattan, we were shaken by the terrorist attacks of September 11, 2001. No matter what our politics, however, our military actions in Afghanistan have left us all worried about reprisals of uncertain potency. The introduction of anthrax into the postal system, the origin of which still eludes police, left us worried to do something as simple, as loving, as to open a letter. And in this congregation, we have been dealing with far more than our share of death and tragedy. If any of us are feeling a little bit ragged, slightly more on edge than we would like, it is completely understandable, even normal. We have gone through a lot, and we still are going through it. My exasperated refrain as of late has been, "When it rains, it pours."

One night recently, I found myself shouting into the air, "O God, deliver me!" I wanted all this frenetic activity to cease, to have just a brief reprieve from everything that was cascading upon on us as a nation, as a congregation, in my family, and among my friends. I wanted to call, "Time out!"

But that, of course, is impossible to do. Life happens, and it is up to us to find the means to keep up with whatever it throws our way. And so what I found myself praying for, instead, was a time of deliverance. I wanted God to alleviate these difficult circumstances, to make it all better. At the very least, I wanted God to grant me just a little grace, a little endurance, a spark more of energy, so that I could do all that I needed to do to get by. I didn't want merely to *survive* through these times but to *thrive* in the middle of them.

And then it occurred to me that what I was feeling and saying in my prayers was nothing other than what goes on in the Psalms. Sometimes the psalmists relate thanks for what God has done to protect them, but they also cry out to God for strength, endurance, deliverance:

> Do not, O Lord, withhold your mercy from me;
> let your steadfast love and your faithfulness keep me
> safe forever.
> For evils have encompassed me without number;
> my iniquities have overtaken me, until I cannot see;
> they are more than the hairs of my head, and my
> heart fails me.
> Be pleased, O Lord, to deliver me;
> O Lord, make haste to help me. (Ps. 40:11–13)

Is it a little over the top for us to pray that "evils have encompassed me without number"? Yes, but that's the point. This psalm is the very real rhetoric of someone who is grasping for deliverance.

And what follows is even more realistic: "My iniquities have overtaken me, until I cannot see ... and my heart fails me." We all know that feeling, we have all gone through moments when we felt overwhelmed by everything that is happening, by everything that we have had to endure. In the worst of those moments, the idea flashes into our minds, "I don't know if I have the strength or desire to continue. It's all become too much. If I just let go, I can be free of all these demands, all this pain." Usually, we can shake off such fatalistic sensibilities, but sometimes, just sometimes, they linger with us longer than we want.

At that moment, we come to a crossroad. And more often than not, how we navigate that treacherous terrain is dependent on how we see ourselves in the world, how we understand the very basis of our identity. If we look at ourselves and see only flesh and bone that encounters the world alone, drawing only on its own skill, savvy, determination, and will, in the end we shall fail. Life and loss will overcome us. It's the sin of utter self-reliance, the belief that we can survive anything. And it's just not true. Our self-reliance can betray us and leave us helpless.

The alternative is to see ourselves as needing something more than what we can provide on our own. It is to have the courage to admit that we are vulnerable, that we need other people, to let others into our hearts, our homes, our very lives. It requires trust, and it means that we risk being hurt. But it is also an occasion for hope, as we invite others to do more than know who we are—to shape, change, transform us. Through their influence, we bloom into someone beyond who we are now or could ever become by ourselves.

The same is true with God. We must be willing to receive God into our hearts, our homes, our very lives. Although it might be a theologically scandalous thing to say, it is pastorally correct: God needs us to be open in order to have any positive impact on our lives. Sometimes, when we are in pain, when we trudge through difficult times, our own concerns scream so loudly that we can't hear God's subtle reassurances and affirmations of our value and hope for the future. And so we feel abandoned, betrayed, left alone. If, even in the midst of our great sadness, we allow ourselves the possibility that God might be reaching out to us—despite God's apparent silence—we might hear that still, quiet voice that is God's encouragement and support.

Keeping ourselves open to God and to others is not an easy thing. To do so is to expose our raw spots to even greater damage. But if we do not, our ability to heal is compromised. If we stay all closed up to the possibilities of friendship and love, then only we are truly responsible for any sense of abandonment.

This truth is articulated beautifully in "Where The Streets Have No Name," a song by the remarkable Irish rock band, U2. I remember hearing the song for the first time back in 1987, during the band's concert in Philadelphia. The pulse of the arena had been throbbing fast, waiting eagerly for the concert to begin. But the energy of the vast crowd shifted as the voice of The Edge's silvery guitar began a new song, an instrumental soliloquy that hushed us and bade us listen rather than merely react. Then the words began, sung by Bono, who on that night stood with one arm in a sling, his shoulder dislocated from a fall the week before. The fragile eloquence of the lyrics was made only more poignant by the image of the broken man before us.

"Where The Streets Have No Name" is a song with a conflicted heart and conflicting voices. Depending on how you listen to the song, it may seem at first that there are two people singing plaintively to each other. At second glance, the song may be an interior conversation, two voices within a single person struggling with love and loss amidst an unending need. The song was inspired by Bono's visit to Ethiopia with his wife, Alison Stewart, where they saw relief workers struggling and the terrible divide between the wealthy urbanites and their brothers and sisters who were left to die in the desert. The streets that have no name might be the makeshift roads of the refugee camp, with ramshackle tents strewn on either side, or the Belfast streets, too numerous to name, that have witnessed centuries of bloodshed. Or perhaps the song refers to a new heaven and a new earth where the streets, paved with gold, bear no names.

I want to run
I want to hide
I want to tear down the walls
That hold me inside
I want to reach out
And touch the flame
Where the streets have no name

The opening lyrics are almost painful to hear, with their overwhelming struggle between a fear to love, and bound within them an unquenched desire to embrace love bravely. Is love enough to right the wrongs? Can love be answered only in rejection? Will all this expenditure of will and energy still lead, in the end, to death? The response to this struggle is to claim a human future of hope. It is a cry of the destitute to embrace their humanity, to live lives that are rich and no longer bound in despair, an appeal toward an improbable future, a denial of the inescapable. And it is a prophetic "No!" to those who would stop helping just because of the enormity of the challenge.

> Where the streets have no name
> Where the streets have no name
> Still building
> Then burning down love
> Burning down love
> And when I go there
> I go there with you
> (It's all I can do)

U2's refrain reminds us that in the midst of our vulnerability, it is the company of others that our identity is forged and our authenticity is realized. The mutuality at the end of the song refuses the solitary fear of the beginning: in the end, identity must be claimed, with the two voices of the song as one, refusing to be alone anymore.

"Where The Streets Have No Name" is a clarion call to us that we should be bold. We must not be willing to suffer through quiet lives of discontent. While we may go through times when it is entirely appropriate to be sad and bereft, it is *never* the case that we are alone. All around us in our churches and communities there are people who are willing to reach out, hold our hand, embrace us, and watch over us—but only if we are brave enough to tell them that we need help. But even more than that, God is *always* at our side, ready to come through when we most need that help.

Scarsdale Congregational Church
Scarsdale, New York
January 2002

Bridging the Betweens

Raewynne J. Whiteley

Song reference: "Peace on Earth"
Biblical References: Isaiah 2:1-5; Matthew 24:37-44

The word of the Lord to Isaiah: "Many peoples shall come and . . . they shall beat their swords into ploughshares, and their spears into pruning hooks; nation shall not lift up sword against nation, neither shall they learn war any more."

> Heaven on earth
> we need it now
> I'm sick of all this
> Hanging around
> Sick of sorrow
> Sick of pain
> Sick of hearing
> again and again
> That there's gonna be
> Peace on earth.

A city street, and a man stands on a bus, clutching a ticket in his sweaty hand. Then a searing fireball, twisted metal and cold silence.

> Heaven on earth
> we need it now

A cathedral chapel, towers of black metal rise from a tray of concrete dust, and candles stand sentinel over the names of the dead: John, Allison, David, Shawn, Colleen, Donnie, Sal...

> Heaven on earth
> we need it now

There's dust on the ground, hard packed like stone, and on it two large toes bound with a dirty white rag, a beaten body receding into nameless death.

> Heaven on earth
> we need it now

U2's song seems to capture the place that we are in right now. Standing in a hotel lobby yesterday, I saw Christmas decorations and heard Christmas carols playing: "Silent night, holy night, all is calm, all is bright"; and part of me wanted to shout *No! No!* Nothing is calm, nothing is bright! I turn on the TV, and twenty-something people have been killed, mostly young adults, in Israel, and in the Palestinian West Bank two children have been shot dead, and the day before a family died in Afghanistan when an aid package fell on their house, and the day before and the day before and the day before....

All is calm, all is bright? What are we doing, heading toward Christmas with its talk of peace and its haloed baby in a manger, what are we doing reading Isaiah with its promises of nations coming together and melting their armaments to make farm tools, when war seems to be escalating, and terror increasing, when all around us is fear and broken promises and death?

It is Advent, and I sometimes wonder if we know what we are doing. I guess, if I had my choice, I'd put aside the war and the pain and the difficulty and run with the baby Jesus and peace and joy, because that's what life is all about, or at least that's the fairy tale that we want to believe in. We want the world to be a good place, a place where we are safe and loved and happy, where life is good and babies are typical in their innocence instead of extraordinary. That's the dream, that's the illusion of Christmas. That's why, as soon as Thanksgiving is over, we put up the decorations and turn on the carols. And if I had my choice, I'd really rather our gospel reading for today had begun where it should, with the beginning of the story of Jesus in the first few verses of Matthew. But if we're honest, we all know that it's an escape, an illusion, and real life is a whole lot more sordid, and perhaps the people who put our lectionary together knew better than we do that what we need at this time is not an injection of fairy tale but an injection of reality in all its grimy anguish. And so, juxtaposed with Isaiah's promise of peace is Jesus' prediction of pain. He returns us to the days of Noah, days not known for their glory but lamented for their depravity. This time between Christ's earthly life and his return, this time between promise and fulfillment, will be a time like that of Noah. A time when people were caught up in their own lives and their own interests, when they cared more about the wine they would drink tonight than the beggars lying hungry outside their gates, when they fought for their own importance and laughed at crazy old Noah, giving up everything to follow the call of an unseen God.

It's a lot more like our world than the world of our Christmas cards.

Yes, we dream of peace, yes, we dream of a better time to come, but in the meantime we have to live in the reality of a world torn apart by selfishness and greed and fear. But that reality is not all there is; that reality is not the whole story. For all that we suffer, for all that we struggle, there is also a promise. A promise that one day all this will end. One day God will come, one day Christ will return, one day there will be heaven on earth, or at least earth will be caught up into heaven, and the tables will be turned, good will triumph over evil and right over wrong, and there will be peace, and love, and joy.

But we live in the in-between times. We live knowing the promise but seeing little hope of its fulfillment. We live caught between fear and faith, between history and hope. There is a gap, and the pain and the suffering and the sorrow which are all around us threaten to overwhelm us.

Christmas, at least as the carols and Christmas cards would have us believe, offers us an escape, a refuge from what we see every time we turn on the TV. But an escape can only ever be temporary, and refuge is fine for a time, but eventually we must emerge into the cold light of day, where the reality is that we live in in-between times, times between the promise and the fulfillment, between fear and faith, between history and hope. Advent is about those in-between times, and Advent is where God will meet us.

We have, on the one hand, a world in a mess, and it doesn't seem like there is a whole lot of hope. And on the other hand we have a vision of something better. That has always been the struggle of Advent. Because we are caught, caught in the in-between. Between a haloed baby in a straw-filled manger and angels announcing "Peace on earth," and a bloodied man, on a splintery cross, crying out, "Forgive them, Father. For they do not know what they do." Between a weeping Jesus at the tomb of Lazarus in a small town outside Jerusalem and the heavenly Jerusalem where all tears will be wiped away. Between the fear of a God who comes like a thief in the night and the hope of a God who comes not to steal but to save.

And bridging those betweens is the promise of Easter, the promise of a God who proclaims, "I am the resurrection and the life! Whoever believes in me, even though they die, shall live!" The promise of a God who enters a locked room, holes in his hands and side, and breathes peace on his friends. Who gives bread and wine, body and blood as a foretaste of the heavenly banquet.

Bridging those betweens is Christ, haloed baby in a manger, weeping friend by a four-day-old tomb, dying body croaking forgiveness from a cross, resurrected life offering peace, bright image of God awaiting us in glory.

It's a bridge, this Christ who doesn't solve the problems or remove the ambiguities or the pain or the struggle, but who says that promise will make way for fulfillment, and perhaps fear can be met with faith, and maybe history and hope do rhyme.

And it's a bridge, this Christ who is *our* head and we, the church, his body. So that in our lives, we echo the life of Christ, bridging the betweens. In our bodies the life of Christ resounds, in our spirits, the Spirit of Christ reverberates, ringing out his tears, his forgiveness, his peace, his resurrection, in our world.

Heaven on earth . . .

Episcopal Church of St Michael and St George
St Louis, Missouri
2 December 2001

part 3

staring
at the
sun

*They said of Abba Macarius the Great
that he became, as it is written, a god upon
earth, because, just as God protects the world,
so Abba Macarius would cover the faults
which he saw, as though he did not see them;
and those which he heard, as though he did
not hear them.*

— Sayings of the Desert Fathers[1]

You don't have to look far to see darkness.

People of violence on both sides of every ocean talk of taking earthly kingdoms by force for heaven, and satellites beam their words into our living rooms. There's a smoking hole in the city, in the countryside. There's emptiness in a house on the block, a space at the table, blank eyes in the despairing human being who brushes past me on the street. Those eyes unsettle more than anything else; they remind me of a cold and vacant place inside me that I thought was healed.

You look into the distance. Look outside. Look up. That's where the light is, and it's bathing me and you, everyone who's afraid and everyone we're afraid of, running over us like the honey of the promised land, binding us together. It's enough.

There are different kinds of darkness, of blindness. There is the darkness of knowing hatred and despair in the world, in your neighbor, and in yourself. There is the darkness of refusing to face what you know, of settling for lies, fumbling with fingers too numb to feel because feeling would be too painful. And then there is the darkness Abba Macarius saw, neither hiding from the real woundedness before him nor settling for a quiet despair that may be superficially comforting in its familiarity, but staring at the sun, looking for the light beyond and within the dark, surrendering to the cloud of unknowing that we experience when bathed in light too bright to see.

You're not the only one looking.

Sarah Dylan Breuer

---

1 *The Sayings of the Desert Fathers: The Alphabetical Collection,* trans. Benedicta Ward, SLG, (Kalamazoo, MI: Cistercian Publications, 1975), 113.

Reconcilers in a Violent World

Jay R. Lawlor

Song reference: "Sunday Bloody Sunday"

Biblical references: John 20:1-9, Ephesians 2:13-17

On January 30, 1972 I was almost two years old and living an ocean away from the island nation of Ireland. On that day, thirteen civilian demonstrators in Derry, Ireland were shot and killed by British Army soldiers, and one demonstrator later died from wounds suffered that day. The British soldiers contended that they were fired upon first, while survivors of the demonstration and victims' families have always stated that the protestors were unarmed. The day became known as Bloody Sunday and became a chapter in Northern Ireland's violent conflict. At age two, I was unaware of the struggles across the Atlantic Ocean, but eleven years later U2 would make the tragedy of that day vivid in my teenage mind, causing me to ask many questions about such conflicts and the response of my Christian faith.

In "Sunday Bloody Sunday," Bono sings the lament so familiar in the tradition of many psalms:

> I can't believe the news today
> Oh, I can't close my eyes
> And make it go away

How long
How long must we sing this song?

Like the prophets I read about in Sunday School, U2 set
before me the violent struggles of their nation and held in
contrast God's reconciling love, the same reconciling love
that we see in the story of the resurrection in John 20:1–9, as
Jesus overcomes death on the cross and God, through Christ,
gives us the opportunity to claim that victory.

But we need to live into that reconciling act. And that is
the message of Ephesians 2:13–17. Christ's blood has brought
two groups together as one in Christ. Through Christ's reconciling act, hostility is replaced with love and divisions
cease, allowing humanity to be reconciled to God and to one
another. The message to the Christian community in
Ephesus, and to us, is that Christ came proclaiming peace.
Yet, we know all too well that our world is divided by oppression and violent conflict.

Like the letter to the Ephesians, U2 points to a new
humanity through Christ where love, peace and reconciliation replace hatred, brutality, and division. Bono sings that
he can't make the violent, bloody images of that Sunday go
away. The images of "broken bottles under children's feet"
and "bodies strewn across a dead end street" are forever
imprinted in his mind. But he also sings of an alternative:

But I won't heed the battle call
It puts my back up
Puts my back up against the wall

Violence only backs us into a corner. Answering a battle
call of conflict only results in a spiraling downward into a
never-ending cycle of heaping violent acts upon violent acts.
As Christians we are called to meet injustice and violence
with forgiveness, prayer, and blessings (Lk. 6:27–28).

There's many lost but tell me who has won
The trenches dug within our hearts
And mother's children, brothers, sisters
Torn apart

Violent battle is not "the real battle" for Christians and such conflict has no real winners. In violent conflict many lose their lives, hearts grow cold as hate crowds out love, and families are shattered. In the tradition of the psalmist U2 laments the hatred and bloodshed: "How long?" Jesus is calling us to another way. Jesus instructs us to be at peace with one another, to obey the great commandment to love one another, and to love our enemies. God has reconciled us to Godself and has given us the ministry of reconciliation: we can be as one! Whatever divisions humanity has created are to be dealt with peacefully and reconciled because of God's selfless act of love for the world. Violent conflicts are not of God's making or God's will, but of humanity's failings. Because of Christ, we can be as one. We don't have to wait for God's reign to be fully realized: We can be as one right now, if we choose to follow the path of love, peace, and reconciliation. "Wipe your tears away. Wipe your bloodshot eyes."

The song continues with a plea that the hostility will end, that the tears will be wiped from the eyes of those who suffer and mourn (Rev. 7:9–17), that we will know God's just reign now. But it will not happen without our help. As God's reconcilers, it is our job to proclaim Christ's message of peace and reconciliation and to wipe away the tears of hatred and violence, so that blood no longer flows on our battlefields and in our streets.

Yet in order to be God's reconcilers, we must be paying attention to the conflicts and struggles of the world. We cannot avert our eyes and hope that they will somehow go away. We cannot shelter ourselves in our homes or our churches and live our lives as if nothing is happening or as if these struggles are someone else's problem.

> And it's true we are immune
> When fact is fiction and TV reality
> And today the millions cry
> We eat and drink while tomorrow they die

We make ourselves immune by accepting fiction as the reality we want to create for ourselves. We gather around our dinner tables in the evening, and focus our attention anywhere but with how we deal with the problems of the world, and tomorrow those problems claim more lives. We attend our churches and gather around the Eucharistic table to eat holy bread and drink holy wine, but forget that this is not the totality of Christian life—it is the spiritual nourishment we need for our engagement as the Church, the Body of Christ in the world, spiritual nourishment to proclaim Christ's peace and reconciling love.

"Sunday Bloody Sunday" is about a tragic day in Ireland's history. But like Scripture, it reveals a universal message about human conflict and God's reconciling love. It's a message that cries out to be heard amid the violence in Israel and Palestine, the ethnic cleansing of Bosnia, genocide in Rwanda, war with Iraq, gang violence on city streets, terrorism, and numerous other oppressions and acts of violence that humans inflict upon one another. There are many ways in which we are called to participate in acts of reconciliation, and in an increasingly global society our action, or inaction, has an impact in places we may never even visit.

And this fact should make us ever more mindful of the reconciliation that we are called to in our own everyday lives. We all certainly know and experience the struggles that exist between people in our families, our church, and in the local community. We don't always agree with one another, and we don't even all like one another. Our disagreements and hostility toward each other can lead to hurtful name-calling, petty gossip, slander, and triangulation. Each of these actions builds distrust, hurt, hardness of heart, and separation. If there is any hope of replacing the division and violence of a Bloody Sunday with Christ's reconciliation, we must learn how to live reconciled lives ourselves.

We need to recognize that those with whom we disagree, whom we dislike and who dislike us, are children of God just as we are children of God. Living reconciled lives as children of a God who loves us and calls us to respect each other means that we are truthful about our disagreements and hurts, but that we always speak that truth in love and listen to one another in love. Only then can we move past anger and hurt. We will not always agree with each other, but there is a difference between unity and uniformity. If we are united as children of God, and we listen and speak truth in love, then we can begin to turn from lives of division to lives of reconciliation.

As "Sunday Bloody Sunday" makes clear, "the real battle" for Christians is not a battle of violence but a battle within ourselves, "to claim the victory Jesus won." Christ's death upon the cross and his resurrection broke the bonds of violence, the bonds of death, and that is the message we are called to live. "How long must we sing this song" calling for the end of hatred, violence, and oppression? How long? Until the world knows the love, the peace, the reconciliation, of Sunday, Easter Sunday.

Service for Reconciliation
Grace Episcopal Church
New Bedford, Massachusetts
Spring 2003

Grace: U2, the Apostle Paul, and Latin American Theology

Clint McCann

Song reference: "Grace"
Biblical reference: Romans 5:1–8

This may not be a fair question, but stay with me for a moment: What do the Bible, the rock group U2, and noted teacher and author Henri Nouwen have in common? The answer: They all talk about, or write about, or in U2's case, sing about, *grace*. And not only does U2 sing about grace in their song by that name, but lead singer Bono and U2 are also a wonderful example of what it means *to live by grace*. We desperately need such examples, because in our contemporary U.S. culture, grace has become nearly incomprehensible.

What is grace? Grace is the word that describes the reality that God does not treat people simply according to what they may or may not deserve. Grace means, for instance, that God doesn't punish the guilty! Grace is God's unconditional acceptance of all persons. Knowing that I am an ordained minister, people often ask me, "How can I *deserve* grace?" But this question misses the point entirely. Grace *cannot* be deserved! In biblical terms, grace is God's *unmerited* favor. As the Apostle Paul puts it in Romans 5:8, "But God proves his love for us in that while we still were sinners Christ died for us." It's not fair! And it is precisely this unfairness that makes grace so hard to comprehend in our merit-oriented, achievement-obsessed culture.

This is exactly why Henri Nouwen concluded that he literally had to leave the United States in order to learn finally what grace and gratitude are truly all about. Nouwen went to Bolivia and Peru, and in the conclusion to his book *Gracias! A Latin American Journal,* he issues "A Call to Be Grateful" in these words:

> In many of the families I visited nothing was certain, nothing predictable, nothing totally safe. Maybe there would be food tomorrow, maybe there would be work tomorrow, maybe there would be peace tomorrow. Maybe, maybe not . . . . What I claim as a right, my friends in Bolivia and Peru received as a gift; what is obvious to me was a joyful surprise to them; what I take for granted, they celebrate in thanksgiving; what for me goes by unnoticed became for them a new occasion to say thanks.
>
> And slowly I learned. I learned what I must have forgotten somewhere in my busy, well-planned, and very "useful" life. I learned that everything that is, is freely given by the God of love. All is grace. Light and water, shelter and food, work and free time, children, parents, grandparents, birth and death—it is all given to us. Why? So that we can say gracias, thanks: thanks be to God, thanks to each other, thanks to all and everyone.[2]

Taking Nouwen as inspiration and example, I have in recent years taken every opportunity to visit Latin America. One of the persons I have met there is Elsa Tamez, a New Testament scholar and former president of the Latin American Biblical University in San José, Costa Rica. She has written a book called *The Amnesty of Grace: Justification by Faith*

2 *Gracias! A Latin American Journal* (Maryknoll, NY: Orbis, 1983/1993), 187–188.

from a Latin American Perspective, in which she attempts to explain the profound implications of a text like Romans 5:1-8 and its invitation to live by "this grace in which we stand" (v. 2). In the book's preface, Tamez states her concern that the contemporary world-situation "allows no room for grace." Furthermore, she is convinced that Paul's message of justification (that is, God's pursuit of justice) "speaks to us of the feasibility of a new logic guided by the power of faith and grace . . . ."[3]

Tamez argues that it is incorrect to reduce justification by grace in Paul to the forgiveness of sins. It does involve this, Tamez suggests, but the forgiveness of sins is aimed at God's ultimate goal of reconciling the world to God's own self (2 Cor. 5:16-21)—that is, of establishing God's justice and righteousness in the world. Paul's logic is simple but has often been missed, according to Tamez, because Paul has been read with an orientation that is too individualistic. To paraphrase Tamez, Paul's logic goes something like this:

Because all have sinned (see Rom. 1-3), no person or group of persons can rightfully claim to be superior or more deserving than other individuals or groups. So, there is no warrant for exclusion, especially exclusion that threatens the very life of others (as is the case regularly when global economic arrangements that benefit North Americans serve to exclude Latin Americans, often threatening their very lives). Thus, those who believe in and live by grace will discern and embody "solidarity," which is the direct result or "root" of justification.[4]

As for the Apostle Paul, his form of "solidarity" involved the radical—indeed, *unthinkable* to many of his contemporaries, including Peter, at first—movement to include the Gentiles in the church (without their first having to become Jews or observe the Torah in traditional terms). For the contemporary North American church, "solidarity" might involve the simple but difficult step of recognizing the poor in Latin America as our brothers and sisters. As Tamez points out, this should regularly happen at the Lord's Table, the celebration that demonstrates conclusively "that grace has a

---

3 *The Amnesty of Grace: Justification by Faith from a Latin American Perspective,* trans. Sharon H. Ringe (Nashville: Abingdon Press, 1993), 7.
4 Ibid.; see especially pp. 134-140.

character that is intrinsically social and communitarian."[5] At this point, Tamez's argument resonates with that of William Placher, who suggests that when the church baptizes and celebrates the Lord's Supper according to Christ's institution, it is acting precisely as "a community of equals and a community of grace."[6] Or, in slightly different terms, Tamez argues that Paul's proclamation of justification by grace finds its functional equivalent in Jesus' proclamation and embodiment of the realm of God, which was and is characterized by concrete expressions "of God's love of the excluded,"[7] such as Jesus' table-fellowship with the outcast and unclean, a way of "eating gracefully" that should be understood in direct continuity with the Lord's Supper.[8]

Needless to say, Jesus' "eating gracefully" and Paul's proclamation and embodiment of the "logic of grace" has changed the world, and it still can! In a recent book, *Revenge: A Story of Hope,* Laura Blumenfeld offers a striking instance of grace in action. Her father, a rabbi from New York, was visiting Jerusalem in 1986 when he was shot and injured by a Palestinian gunman. After this, Laura Blumenfeld vowed to get revenge. In 1998, having become a journalist with *The Washington Post,* Blumenfeld went to Israel to track down information on the crime for the purpose of writing a book on revenge. After meeting the gunman's family and eventually the gunman himself, Blumenfeld's "revenge" turned out to be an appeal for clemency for the imprisoned gunman when, due to his severe illness, his case came up for review in an Israeli court. Neither the gunman nor his family knew Blumenfeld's full identity until the hearing when the judges sought to block her intervention in the case. Only at that point did Laura Blumenfeld assert that she had a right to speak at the hearing, because her father, David Blumenfeld, was one of the gunman's victims.

Reflecting on this dramatic scene and Blumenfeld's dramatic change of heart and mind, reviewer Scott Dalgarno writes:

---

5 Ibid., 139.
6 *Narratives of a Vulnerable God: Christ, Theology, and Scripture* (Louisville: Westminster John Knox Press, 1994), 144.
7 Tamez, *Amnesty of Grace,* 157.
8 Placher, *Narratives of a Vulnerable God,* 137.

This book gives me hope that perhaps one day, years from now, families of the people who died in the Sept. 11, 2001 hijackings and crashes will go to Saudi Arabia and they will sit down with the families of those 19 men who hijacked the four planes. And who knows what might come from such meetings? As Laura Blumenfeld said, "When you really take time to look someone in the eye, it becomes very hard to shoot him in the head."[9]

Who knows, indeed, what might come from such meetings? They could just change the world!

And changing the world is exactly what U2 is about, along with Jesus and Paul and Elsa Tamez and Henri Nouwen and Laura Blumenfeld. In their song "Grace," U2 affirms that grace is "a thought that changed the world" because "grace finds goodness in everything" and "beauty in everything."

Theologian Douglas John Hall defines the mission of the church in exactly the same terms that U2 uses to describe grace:

The goal of mission is nothing more or less than this: to participate in our Lord's mission to help creation discover and realize the LIFE that is being offered in the midst of all this death. To help God "change the world."[10]

It is highly significant, of course, that U2 not only *sings* about grace as a reality that changes the world, they also *live* by grace, participating actively in helping the world reorient

---

9 A review of *Revenge: A Story of Hope* (Simon And Schuster, 2002) in *The Presbyterian Outlook* 184/39 (Nov. 18, 2002), 2.

10 *Christian Mission: The Stewardship of Life in the Kingdom of Death* (New York: Friendship Press, 1985), 98. For further discussion of Hall's definition of mission, see Darrell W. Cluck, Catherine S. George, and J. Clinton McCann, Jr., *Facing the Music: Faith and Meaning in Popular Songs* (St. Louis: Chalice Press, 1999), 113–117. This volume is, like the present volume, an attempt to explore how contemporary music can be used in relation to the proclamation of the gospel.

itself to the life that God offers. U2's solidarity with the needy in Africa can be traced to Live Aid in 1985. Bono has worked incognito in a relief camp in Ethiopia, and he played a major role in Jubilee 2000, an international movement to aid the poor by seeking debt relief for developing nations in Africa and Latin America. U2's web page includes links to the charities and humanitarian causes that they support, including Amnesty International, nuclear disarmament, and AIDS research, which received all the royalties from one of their biggest hits on *Achtung Baby.*

Not too long after the release of the CD that contains the song "Grace," Bono was continuing his longstanding efforts in Africa. He was traveling with U.S. Treasury Secretary Paul O'Neill, whom he had persuaded to go with him to witness the devastation and death. Bono's hope was that O'Neill might also be persuaded to use his influence to lead the U.S. toward more extensive and compassionate engagement to meet the needs of African countries and their people—in short, to change the world.

At an AIDS clinic in Soweto, South Africa (a country where AIDS infects nearly 25 percent of the population!), Bono spoke the following words, words that reveal grace's ability to find "goodness in everything" and "beauty in everything": "This is an amazing place, amazing people . . . . Our lives have been blessed by meeting you people today, and I will never, ever forget it."[11] Not coincidentally, the adjective "amazing" is one that many people associate with the word "grace," on account of the beloved hymn, "Amazing Grace." U2's song and Bono's words invite us to consider the challenging possibility that the *most* amazing thing about grace is its ability to enable us to see goodness and beauty in everything, even

---

11 Quoted in a report from The Associated Press in the *St. Louis Post-Dispatch,* Sunday, May 26, 2002. For information on other ways that Bono has been and is involved in, in effect, changing the world, see, for instance, Josh Tyrangiel, "Bono: The World's Biggest Rock Star is also Africa's Biggest Advocate, but Bono Knows He has to Make the Case for Aid with his Head, Not his Heart," *Time* 159 (March 4, 2002), 62ff.; "U2's Spiritual Journey Defies Categorizing," *The Christian Century* 119 (Feb. 13, 2002), 12; Anthony DeCurtis, "Bono's Crusade," *Rolling Stone* (March 14, 2002), 25.

in people we might chose to ignore and places we'd rather forget. And therein lies the hope of changing the world!

Sardis Presbyterian Church
Charlotte, North Carolina
22 February 2002

Living the Question:
Privilege, Poverty, and Faith

Jennifer M. McBride

Song reference: Concert material between "Bad" and
"Where the Streets Have No Name" from
Elevation 2001/U2: Live from Boston
Biblical references: Isaiah 58:6–8,11; Matthew 19:24

How long? How long?" echoes U2's familiar mantra, as the band transitions in Boston's FleetCenter from "Bad" to "Where the Streets Have No Name." How long—a phrase with which U2 ends their song based on Psalm 40—how long must we sing these songs that grapple with the reality of human suffering? How long until what is wrong will be made right?

"I want to beg you as much as I can to be patient towards all that is unsolved in your heart and to try to love the questions themselves," the poet Rainer Maria Rilke writes, as if in response to these questions. "The point is to live everything—live the questions now. Perhaps you will then gradually, without noticing it, live along some distant day into the answer."[12]

---

12 Rainer Maria Rilke, *Letters to a Young Poet*, trans. M.D. Herter Norton (London: Norton, 1993).

I have questioned in depth two aspects of my life—my privilege and my Christian faith. And my questions involving one often influence the other. After graduating from college, I worked for two years at the Southeast White House, a house serving an impoverished inner-city community in Washington, D.C., just four miles from the U.S. Capitol Building. There especially, the tension between American privilege and poverty consumed my thoughts, and I began to ask hard questions within a Christian theological framework about the complex reality of poverty. In my naiveté, I used to think that I was basically impoverished, when compared to my peers, because my father is a high school teacher, not a doctor or lawyer, my mother is a secretary, and I grew up in a small apartment in Probasco Hall.[13] And so in pride and self-righteousness, I thought that I was exempt from certain attitudes and perspectives that can come from wealth and privilege.

I am, however, extremely privileged. I am what David Hilfiker calls "irredeemably middle-class." Hilfiker is a doctor in Washington, D.C. He runs a medical clinic named Christ House that serves homeless men, and he lives with his family in an apartment above the clinic. He says:

> There are privileges of birth and upbringing I could never renounce, even if I wanted to. I could give away all my money, but none of my education. . . . I could renounce the trappings of privilege . . . but—were I ever in desperate need—my parents or my siblings or my church community or my friends (all with solid, middle-class resources) would be present to bail me out. No matter how poor I became, I would always have the connections that promise me a security unknown to those in the ghetto. And were all of the above taken away, I would still have a life-long sense of entitlement to fall back on. . . . No matter what happens to me in the future, I will never share the experiences of grow-

13 Probasco Hall is a boy's dormitory on The Baylor School's campus. My father was a professor there until recently, and he and my mother were dorm parents for almost twenty-five years.
14 David Hilfiker, *Not All of Us Are Saints: A Doctor's Journey With the Poor* (New York: Hill and Wang, 1994), 78-79.

ing up poor and powerless within the abusive environment of the inner city.[14]

You and I are privileged beyond measure. When I began questioning my own privilege, I found that my abundance of material and situational riches impaired my ability to understand the true character of Jesus' life. In high school and much of college, my faith focused on Jesus' sacrificial death, and I thought that this perspective alone was the key to understanding the mystery of God and humanity. But I have discovered that it is quite difficult for a privileged person to be poor in spirit or humble, to admit need, to acknowledge that she has a false sense of control over her life: I am the one to whom Jesus refers when he says that "it is easier for a camel to go through the eye of a needle than for someone who is rich to enter the Kingdom of God" (Mt. 19:24).

To be poor materially is to have little or nothing that is your own, to be needy, powerless, perhaps to have a hunger from an empty stomach. I think of a five-year-old boy, Delante, who lives across the street from the Southeast White House. One early summer afternoon, Delante showed up in the kitchen when I happened to be walking through, and with a look empty of pretense said, "Miss Jenny, can I have some potato chips?" I am sure there were previous similar encounters in which I simply told him or another child that he couldn't have the chips, but this day I stopped and asked if he had eaten lunch. He said he hadn't. I asked if he had eaten breakfast; again, he had not. Then I asked if his mother was at home. He told me that she was, so I said, "Delante, how about you go home and tell your mom that you are hungry, and I bet she'll give you some food." But Delante replied, "She's home but she locks all the doors."

I later wept over that interaction, over my past hastiness, over previously not knowing the right questions to ask, over Delante's need. I wept that situations exist in which a mother, intending the best for her young children, locks them out of the house in the morning instead of exposing them to what goes on inside. Delante's world was almost incomprehensible to me.

This moment with Delante was significant because, although I had been working in the neighborhood for months, it was the first time that I truly allowed another person's pain and suffering to invade my well-ordered and rather simple world. I also saw, in Delante, who I am to be. He said, "I'm hungry, I need, I'm powerless. I cannot get food unless you give it to me." His humility, his lowly position before me defined him in that moment. I *too* am hungry, needy, and ultimately powerless and poor before my God, whether I admit it or not, whether I live like it or not.

So I am privileged and I am poor. What can I do with this tension and with the discrepancy between my overabundance of privilege and another person's poverty? One response to these tensions is to live in the awareness that all that I have is not my own—it is God's—and to live sacrificially in gratitude and continuous service.

Amidst these same tensions, and with the question of "how long, how long to sing this song of suffering, of inhumane poverty?" filling a Boston stadium, Bono asks, "What can I give back to God for the blessings he poured out on me? What can I give back to God for the blessings he poured out on me? I lift high the cup of salvation, raise a toast to our Father—follow through on the promise I made to you." He speaks these words as "Where the Streets Have No Name" begins—a song about, on at least one level, the Kingdom of God coming to earth in its fullness. It is a song of longing and confident hope. The members of U2 embody their own words and live within their questions by using U2's privileged platform to fight globally against poverty and injustice.

The late Abraham Heschel, a prominent Jewish theologian who worked with Martin Luther King, Jr. during the Civil Rights era, said about injustice and oppression, "In a free society, some of us are guilty but all are responsible."[15] The responsibility to which Heschel refers includes being in relationship with the poor. I have learned that I am to so concentrate on other people's needs that I do not worry about my own, knowing that I have a good and faithful God who provides for me and who promises me my daily bread. We have or will have resources such as education, money, and social power to share.

---

15 Susannah Heschel, "Theological Affinities in the Writings of Abraham Joshua Heschel and Martin Luther King, Jr." in *Black Zion: African American Religious Encounters With Judaism*, ed. Yvonne Chireau and Nathaniel Deutsch (Oxford: Oxford University Press, 2000).

Perhaps even more importantly, we as people of privilege need to be in relationship with people who are impoverished. We need them to expose to us that something is deeply wrong. We need them to move us toward a confession that we indeed are poor, and that we all too often care only for ourselves. It took approximately one week working in an inner-city neighborhood to shatter my romantic notions about working with the poor for peace and justice and for racial and socioeconomic reconciliation. We need interactions and relationships with those who are poor right here in Chattanooga, so that these interactions might produce in us what Martin Luther King called "creative tension"—that unsettledness that leads to awareness and actions whose goal is peace, justice, and reconciliation.

As humans, what we do alone is done in vain. Real socioeconomic and political change can and does take place, especially from a grassroots perspective; however, change is nothing without the mysterious presence and power and grace of God. And God is concerned with our physical and communal existence: God became a human being; the Word of God, Jesus Christ, became flesh. Christian spirituality is surprisingly earthbound. In the Old Testament, God says through the prophet Isaiah:

> Is not this the fast [or the spirituality] that I choose:
> to loose the bonds of injustice
>
> to share your bread with the hungry,
> and bring the homeless poor into your house;
> when you see the naked, to cover them,
> and not to hide yourself from your own kin?
> Then your light shall break forth like the dawn,
> and your healing shall spring up quickly;
>
> The Lord will guide you continually,
> and satisfy your needs in parched places,
> and make your bones strong;
> and you shall be like a watered garden,
> like a spring of water, whose waters never fail.
> (Isa. 58:6–8,11)

While working at the Southeast White House in D.C., I became close to a woman named Kimberly. Our deep friendship defied socioeconomic and racial boundaries. She (unfairly of course) could be reduced to the stereotypical inner-city black welfare mom: single with three children; living in Section 8 housing; drug dealers swarming around her apartment steps. And this was the only reality she had ever known. I (unfairly as well) could be reduced to a white, sheltered, overly optimistic yuppie. Kim considered transferring her Section 8 housing voucher here to Chattanooga to escape from family chaos and the D.C. inner city. So she and I and her baby, David Emmanuel, who by becoming my godson grafted me into her family for life, took a road trip to Chattanooga. When we arrived in town and visited a government project in which she was eligible to live, I became aware that I had new eyes. In high school, if I ever had a thought about the people living in the project, it was no more than a passing thought—I could not comprehend how someone could flourish there. But with Kim that day, what I saw was well-kept green grass, friendly neighbors on their front steps enjoying the sun, spring weather, and one another.

Because of my friendship with Kim, the housing project in Chattanooga no longer felt so alien. That night we stood on Probasco's porch under the moonlight and shared about our childhoods. What I realized then was that walls were broken down by our friendship. Kim belonged in my world, too, here at Baylor. The fortified walls between our worlds are real but not impenetrable. The walls are manufactured, and the consequent isolation injures us all.

My hope is that we will ask the difficult questions about our own lives and about the society we comprise: From where does our privilege come and what is our purpose? How long must we wait before all that is wrong is made right? And as we ask these questions, I hope we will begin to see the world around us with new eyes, and that our perspective will broaden to include both the poor *and* the God who labors on their behalf.

The Baylor School
Chattanooga, Tennessee
10 May 2002

Walk On: Biblical Hope and U2

Brian J. Walsh

Song references: "Sunday Bloody Sunday,"
"Where the Streets Have No Name," "Walk On"
Biblical references: Psalm 13, Revelation 21:1–7, John 14:1–4

Then I saw a new heaven and a new earth . . . I saw the holy city, the new Jerusalem, coming down out of heaven from God . . . See, the home of God is among mortals . . . See, I am making all things new." In the book of Revelation, these are the things that the writer, John, sees.

But what do we see? Do we see newness in the midst of our crumbling empire of military arrogance? Do we see a holy city in the urban collapse all around us? Do we see God at home in the midst of our upper class nomadism and our impoverished homelessness? What do we see?

Christian discipleship requires a clear vision of both the brokenness of our own personal and cultural lives, and of where God is at work to bring healing in the midst of that brokenness. We need vision to see through the media smoke screen, the political doubletalk, and the corporate manufacturing of reality. We need a sharpening of our sight. We need the kind of prophetic and apocalyptic vision that we meet in St. John. And we need help.

One of the places I think we can turn to for such help, for the sharpening of our sight, indeed, for a prophetic and apocalyptic vision, is the music and lyrics of the Irish rock band, U2. Simply stated, U2 is the most successful and biggest rock band in history. And they are, I believe, one of the most powerful witnesses to the Kingdom of God of our day. Taking their name from a Cold War spy plane, this is a band committed to reconnoitering the cultural landscape in order to assess the ethos of our culture and the shifting spirits of our time, and to discern the movement of the Spirit of God in our midst.

U2 comes out of the punk rock scene of the late 1970s *and* a charismatic Christian community in Dublin. As such, they are indebted to the Sex Pistols and Jeremiah, the Ramones and Jesus. And when they began as a band, they announced both publicly and privately that they were simply going to be the best rock band in the world.

But this was not just a matter of Irish adolescent bravado. Rather, the three Christian members of the band believed that God himself had given them the gifts to make a profound impact through their music on the world for the Kingdom of God. In a letter to his father, the lead singer, Bono, wrote about beginning each day in prayer, scripture reading, and inviting God to work in their lives. "This," he wrote, "gives us our strength and a joy that does not depend on drink or drugs. This strength will, I believe, be the quality that will take us to the top of the music business—where never before have so many lost and sorrowful people gathered in one place pretending they're having a good time. It is our ambition to make more than good music."[16] And it is for the lost and the sorrowful that they sing so much of hope.

Hope, as we meet it in U2, is a decidedly this-worldly hope. It is a deep longing for a world that is better than the one that we presently inhabit, a longing, in the words of Hebrews, for that "better country," that "homeland" (Heb. 10:14,16). But it is not what we traditionally think of as heaven. This heaven we long for is not just an eternal destiny—living with Jesus in some ethereal place decidedly different from earth. It is heaven on earth—a restored life with the Lord in a new earth.

Such is the longing that we find in U2, a longing that is shared with the biblical witness: Out of death will come res-

16 Bill Flanagan, *U2 at the End of the World* (New York: Delacorte Press, 1995; reprint, New York: Dell Publishing, 1996), 524.

urrection; grief will be turned to joy; mourning will become dancing; tears will give way to laughter; isolation, loss, and loneliness will be reconciled in a reunion and a festival of friends; war and the empire of violence will be replaced by a Kingdom of shalom; swords will transformed into ploughshares; evil will be vanquished by good; hatred overthrown by love; and the tensions, ambiguities and dead ends of the world's story will finally come to their resolution in the story of our God and of his Christ. It is a longing for a better place, a better country.

But the particular shape that such longing takes is always historically mediated. *Whose* death? *What* grief and mourning? *Whose* tears, loss, and brokenness? *Which* wars, *what* violence, and *which* swords, Molotov cocktails, missiles, or suicide bombers? *What* particular historical evil? Hatred against *whom*? The tensions in *whose* story, at *which* stage or chapter of the world's story? You see, how we conceive of the Kingdom, the shape that hope takes in our lives, is always rooted in our historical and geographical time and place. While hope for some sort of timeless heaven unrelated to this earth can be rather generic and captured in pious platitudes, a biblical hope in the coming Kingdom of God will always take on particular shape because this is a hope that is precisely for *this* world in all of its brokenness, sin, folly, and idolatry, at this *time* in history.

U2 knows this as well as anyone. They were raised in Ireland in the 60s and 70s. Ireland—a place of violence between Protestants and Catholics that has brought nothing but shame to the name of Jesus. It is this violence that is reflected in their song, "Sunday Bloody Sunday" from the 1983 album, *War:*

> Broken bottles under children's feet,
> Bodies strewn across a dead-end street
>
> And the battle's just begun,
> There's many lost, but tell me who has won?
> The trenches dug within our hearts
> And mother's children, brothers, sisters torn apart
>
> Sunday, bloody Sunday.
> Sunday, bloody Sunday.

Can there be hope in a world in which British soldiers fire into crowds of protesters and the Irish Republican Army bombs Protestant communities in Northern Ireland and subways in London? Can there be hope when Sunday—any Sunday—can be a day of murderous bloodshed?

Any hope that is to be biblical must address the realities of violence and hatred in our world and in our own hearts. Maybe we can't believe the news today—news of bombings in Belfast or Jerusalem, terrorist attacks in New York City, or 500,000 children dead because the U.S. deliberately destroyed the water supply infrastructure of Iraq and then imposed sanctions prohibiting the export of chlorine into the country. Maybe we can't believe that politicians will put oil profits over environmental sustainability, or that Africa is being decimated by an AIDS pandemic. And maybe we can't believe that homelessness and abject poverty are realities in our own incredibly wealthy country. We can't believe the news today. But, sings Bono, we can't close our eyes and make it go away. We can't avert our gaze from the deep brokenness of our world. Nor can we simply objectify this brokenness as something "out there" because, the lyrics insist, these trenches of violence and enmity are "dug within our hearts."

And so, in the face of such pain and despair, U2 takes up the refrain of the psalms of lament, "How long, how long must we sing this song?" Our enmity could be transformed into communion; we could be one, even tonight, so how long must we sing this song? This is the heart of biblical hope—the pathos-filled longing and insistence that against all odds and in the face of mounting evidence to the contrary, there can be reconciliation. "Tonight we can be as one." And if that is your hope then you never will play the world's game. Rather, in the face of the violence within and without, and with tears in your own eyes, you will offer to wipe the tears from the eyes of others. This is the only alternative, this is the only hope in a world in which the media numbs us and makes us immune to suffering or, even worse, cheap voyeurs of pain.

But this is a song of hope. The lament, "How long, how long must we sing this song?" is rooted in a hope that U2 expresses in a later song: "Then will there be no time of sorrow, then will there be no time for pain."[17] But in this earlier

---

17 "The Playboy Mansion" from *Pop*, 1997.

song they contrast the battleground of Northern Ireland, indeed the battleground of a world of ethnic, racial, and religious hatred, with a more profound battle of principalities and powers, and battle of the Spirit. The "real battle," sings Bono, is the one "to claim the victory Jesus won on a Sunday, bloody Sunday."

Biblical hope does not avert its gaze from violence. Biblical hope is bought at the cost of the deepest violence of all—the violence of the cross and the victory of a bruised, scarred, and pierced man on a Sunday, a bloody Sunday. Biblical hope, kingdom hope is resurrection hope. And only the Resurrected One can promise a better country. Only the Resurrected One can transform Belfast, New York, Ramallah, Kabul, Bogata, or Baghdad into the New Jerusalem.

"Where the Streets Have No Name" is U2's late twentieth century take on the hope of a New Jerusalem that is found in Revelation 21. After the fall of Babylon—or ancient Jerusalem and Rome or modern Washington and Moscow—after the collapse of all idolatrous cultures and civilizations, the Scriptures still envision a new city, even a heavenly city, but its final abode is not in heaven but on a new and restored earth. In the face of generations upon generations of unfaithfulness, broken covenant, and cultural prostitution, we have here a vision of God's faithfulness from the beginning to the end, a new covenant, a renewal of marriage vows. In this city, the hope of "Sunday Bloody Sunday" is fulfilled. The tears will be wiped from our bloodshot eyes. Instead of broken bottles and bodies strewn across a dead end street, this vision has the audacity to proclaim that "death will be no more; mourning and crying and pain will be no more, for the first things have passed away" (Rev. 21:4).

But the first things have not yet passed away. And so the same artist who sang "I can't close my eyes and make it go away," now sings, "I want to run, I want to hide." He no sooner gives honest voice to the desire to run from pain when he sings:

> I want to tear down the walls
> That hold me inside.
> I want to reach out
> And touch the flame
> Where the streets have no name.

This is, I suggest, both a longing to be set free from those "trenches dug within" our own hearts—those deeply internal forces of self-protection that make us avert our gaze from the pain of the other—and a profound longing for the New Jerusalem. You see, if street names serve to identify what part of town you are from, and in the Irish context whether you are a Protestant or a Catholic, then one's hope for the New Jerusalem will be that it is a place where the streets have no name. It won't matter what side of the tracks you come from, whether you live in a monster-home suburb or in an inner-city single-room occupancy hotel, whether you come from Ramallah or Tel Aviv, Toronto or Tehran, whether you are black, white, yellow, or brown, because in this city, those neighborhoods, addresses, ethnic, class, and national identities are all irrelevant. The dividing walls are broken down, there is neither Greek nor Jew, slave nor free, male nor female, straight nor gay, single nor married, rich nor poor because Christ is all and in all.

In this song we meet a longing for a world no longer threatened by military devastation or ecological ruin.

> I want to feel sunlight on my face
> See that dust cloud disappear without a trace
> I want to take shelter from the poison rain.

But this is a hope that is lived (and here sung) with a deeply realistic grasp on reality. While this place where the streets have no names is grounded and nourished by covenantal love, our reality is that although we attempt to build such a place, such a Kingdom, we nonetheless find that "We're still building / Then burning down love, burning down love." Indeed, this world in its brokenness and idolatry—the city in which we live—is a flood that turns our love to rust. Instead of the flame of the Spirit that we long to touch, in a world where the nuclear dust clouds have disappeared, we find that "we're beaten and blown by the wind" of every new false spirit and cultural force while we are trampled in the dust of our own pollution and cultural ruins.

You see, while John of Patmos envisioned the New Jerusalem in the face of the collapse of the old Jerusalem and the brutality of the Roman empire, U2 of Dublin must dream of a city where the streets have no name in the face of the collapse of the modern project in the bloodstained streets of Belfast and in the dust of the World Trade Center. With apocalyptic vision U2 promises, "I'll show you a place / High on a desert plain / Where the streets have no name." And with a sense of prophetic and covenantal solidarity, U2 proclaims to us and to God, "And when I go there / I go there with you / (It's all I can do)." There is no other recourse. There is no hope for this world other than a new heaven and a new earth, a New Jerusalem coming down out of heaven as a restored cultural reality, a place of peace, renewed community and reconciliation, the dwelling of God amongst us.

So how do we get there? "Walk on," says U2; "walk on." This song was written in honor of the Burmese activist for democracy, Aung San Suu Kyi, who left the security of life with her husband and son at Oxford University to face house arrest under the brutal military junta of her homeland. She walked away from security in search of a better country.

> And love is not the easy thing . . .
> The only baggage you can bring
> Is all that you can't leave behind
>
> And if the darkness is to keep us apart
> And if the daylight feels like it's a long way off
> And if your glass heart should crack
> And for a second you turn back
> Oh no, be strong
>
> Walk on, walk on
> What you got they can't steal it
> No they can't even feel it
> Walk on, walk on
> Stay safe tonight

This is U2's word of hope for those of us who long for heaven on earth, for those of us who seek a better country, a new city, a restoration of this creation that God so lovingly called into being. This is U2's encouragement along the way for those who have packed a suitcase "for a place none of us has been / a place that has to be believed to be seen." Here is their pastoral counsel to those of us who have been singing the lament, "How long must we sing this song?" To those of us who feel that the darkness is keeping us apart and that "the daylight feels like it's a long way off," whose hearts are so fragile that they feel like glass ready to break, they sing, "Walk on." Because what we have—this hope, this longing, this vision of restoration, this imagination of new possibilities—is ours to keep. It cannot be stolen or denied by those who can't even feel it or share it.

This hope is no commodity, no object that can be confiscated by the agents of normality and the status quo in our lives. No, this hope is rooted in a longing for home that beats incessantly in the human heart. So walk on, U2 sings, walk on. Keep your eyes on those promises that you can only see from a distance, on that city prepared for you, that homeland in which there will be no time of sorrow, no time for pain.

And walk on, my friends, walk on. But this is an arduous journey, so you'll have to travel light. In fact, all that you can take, all that you can pack, is a heart—even if it is a glass heart close to shattering—of love. Leave behind "all that you fashion, all that you make," for in the end, this is not a Kingdom that we build, it is a Kingdom established through the radical generosity and love of the King of kings. This Kingdom is not an accomplishment, but a gift.

And when you can walk on with that kind of relinquishment, when you can have the courage to live with that kind of faith, when, just beyond the range of normal sight you can glimpse the goal, the New Jerusalem coming down out of heaven as a bride adorned for her husband, then perhaps you will no longer need to cry "how long must we sing this song?" because your tongues will break into a new song, "Hallelujah, Hallelujah, Hallelujah, Hallelujah."[18]

Student conferences and churches throughout Canada

---

[18] I am indebted to my student Robert Vagacs for opening up new vistas of interpretation of U2's music in his Master of Theological Studies thesis, "The Poet's Voice in Postmodern Culture heard through the Music of U2" (M.T.S. thesis, Wycliffe College, 2002).

part **4**

desire

. . . nowhere is there any final satisfaction,
because nothing there can be defined as
absolutely the best or highest. But it is natural
that nothing should content a man's desires but
the very best, as he reckons it.
— St. Bernard of Clairvaux, *On Loving God* [1]

Therefore
let us desire nothing else
let us wish for nothing else
let nothing else please us
and cause us delight
except our Creator and Redeemer and
Savior . . .
Who alone is Good
merciful and gently
delectable and sweet
— St. Francis of Assisi, *The Earlier Rule* [2]

We are born hungry—voracious, even. We long to take
inside ourselves the nourishment, the heartbeat we experienced in our first awareness as our own. The longing never
leaves. We teach ourselves to hate what (and whom) we

desire—our God, Mother, Lover. We teach ourselves to crave, instead, what we can have, trade bread for bubblegum, domination for desire. But we were born for longing. The universe was born of longing. Love that is not mere narcissism requires an Other; God, being Love, could not be God's self without creating an Other to love. You and I are God's image, born of desire, born to desire. Why do I spend my money for bubblegum instead of bread, working for what will never satisfy? Why, when there is bread and wine and milk without price?[3]

I tell myself that if there is a price, I can earn it, and then I will possess what I desire. But desire is always for the Other. I can try to fill that God-shaped hole; I can convince myself that the shiny, slick things just out of reach and the dizzying giddiness I feel when I touch them are the real thing, or better. Inside, in the darkness most like the darkness in which I first felt a heart beating, I know that what I can possess I can't love, what I can grasp can never fill, what I can find is not what I'm looking for.

And in knowing the longing, I come to know the Love I believe in when the chattering of ambition and acquisition, the booming of the disco, fades to the beat of a heart.

Sarah Dylan Breuer

---

1 St. Bernard of Clairvaux, *On Loving God,* ed. Hugh Martin, trans. W. Harman van Allen (London: SCM Press, 1959), 37.

2 *Francis and Clare: the Complete Works,* trans. Regis J. Armstrong, ofm Cap., and Ignatius C. Brady, ofm (Mahwah, NJ: Paulist Press, 1982), 133.

3 cf. Isaiah 55:1-2.

Pressing On with U2 and Paul

Steve Stockman

Song reference: "I Still Haven't Found What I'm Looking For"
Biblical reference: Philippians 3:1–16

The night that *Joshua Tree* went on sale in March 1987, I rushed out of the Church Youth Group meeting in First Antrim and, in a rush of blood to the head, decided to drive the twenty miles to Belfast to buy the new U2 album that was going on sale at midnight.

The crowds were large and got a little more excited when a car pulled up with all four members of the band inside. They had been in Belfast recording a television show, and we were going to be the lucky people who would have the album signed. I went looking for something else to get signed, other than the album, and came back with my Bible. Larry turned the page over to check the cover and smiled his enigmatic smile, while Bono looked up and said, "That is a great book."

Then it was straight back to my college room to listen to the most anticipated album in quite some time. As always with U2 albums, it took a little time to acclimatize. "Bullet the Blue Sky" seemed uncharacteristically heavy. "Exit" was a weird and haunting piece. Spiritually, too, it was an uneasy beginning. What about "I Still Haven't Found What I'm Looking For"? It seemed a strange dichotomy to have found

Christ and not have found what you are looking for—I went to bed concerned. Was this the renouncing of their faith?

I have been engaged in debate about that song in Africa, Asia, North America, and more times than I can count in my own country. There are so few people, it seems, who get the succinct theology, the searching spirituality, or the vulnerable integrity that sets this song apart from most other attempts at expressing faith in the four minute rock song format. It was U2's producer Daniel Lanois who encouraged Bono to write a "gospel song"—and with a choir in a black church in Harlem, during the filming of *Rattle and Hum,* it became just that.

Biblically, it seems to me that "I Still Haven't Found What I'm Looking For" is set, intentionally or otherwise, in the third chapter of Philippians. Writing to a church in Macedonia, Paul warns against those who would bring legalism back into battle with the grace of the Gospel. The passage is a testimony to what God has done and is doing within Paul's own life. Having attempted to reach God by the perfect legalism of the Pharisee, Paul found another way—a righteousness that comes from God and not from the law (cf. Phil. 3:9). Like Abraham who "believed . . . and it was credited to him as righteousness," (Rom. 4:3 NIV), so Paul finds grace as his way to be justified before God.

In "I Still Haven't Found What I'm Looking For," Bono sings:

> You broke the bonds
> You loosed the chains
> Carried the cross
> And my shame
> And my shame,
> You know I believe it

In just a few lines we find atonement and redemption, economically expressed without ambiguity, followed by a bold declaration of allegiance: "I believe it." In 1992, when U2 had reinvented their persona, all black shiny leather and devil horns, confusing lazy evangelical minds once more, I listened more acutely than ever during their Earl's Court concert on the ZooTV tour. I was keen to get a spiritual temperature check, and it read loud and clear as Bono sang, "You know

I believe it." And then cried, "And I still do!" No denial of faith there.

But it is the next line that always raises doubts: But I still haven't found what I'm looking for.

I remember speaking in Dublin and seeing a rather exuberant Christian at the front of the hall. I began my address by asking if anyone had found what they were looking for. "Amen, brother. Yes! Hallelujah!" he shouted. I am not sure how my dear brother felt as, for the next hour, I explored the idea that to have found what we are looking for has nothing to do with biblical Christianity—not in this life, anyway. To have found what you're looking for actually means you have died and gone to heaven!

As I look at the Middle East, AIDS and poverty decimating the southern countries of Africa, and the continued violence and division in my home city of Belfast, I do not see what I'm looking for. As I look at a Church filled with gossip, malicious lies in the name of truth, guilt-building Pharisees, bigoted hypocrites, I do not see what I'm looking for. As I look into my life and see the egotistical, selfish, sinful husband, son, or friend, I do not see what I'm looking for. Yes, we believe that the cross has changed everything about our lives. But there is so much more to look for.

And so we are back to Philippians 3. After Paul has laid down the credentials of his salvation—all of God and none of himself—he goes on to explain that he has not already arrived. "Not that I have already obtained all this, or have already been made perfect, but I press on to take hold of that for which Christ Jesus took hold of me . . . Forgetting what is behind and straining towards what is ahead, I press on toward the goal to win the prize for which God has called me heavenward in Christ Jesus" (Phil. 3:12–14, NIV). Paul could have phrased it, I still haven't found what I'm looking for.

There are two prongs of God's work of grace. Faith leads us into a position of holiness before God, by Christ's atoning work that very first Easter weekend. Before a holy God, we are declared legally justified. However, we are still practically a long way short of the holiness that the Holy Spirit is then able to bring into our lives. It is the practical holiness that Paul and U2 are striving towards, aware that as they look within and around them it has still not been found.

There is a real temptation just to reach out for salvation with the spiritual hand of faith, and then lie back and wait to be called into heaven. Yet that is not what Jesus died and was raised to life for. We have "an inheritance that can never perish, spoil or fade, kept in heaven for you. . ." (1 Pet. 1:4 NIV), but Jesus' teaching and the entire Scriptures are about much more than our joyous future hope. His death makes possible our death to our old lives; his resurrection brings us into new life and a new world, set free to be transformed into the people that God created and Jesus redeemed us to be. Grace is more than a ticket to the sweet bye-and-bye; it is an engine that makes it possible to pray—and believe and live—the prayer, "Thy kingdom come, thy will be done on earth as it is in heaven."

Bono's lyrics have constantly questioned his own personal walk. He writes of striving to live in the eye of his contradictions—"I don't believe in riches but you should see where I live" ("God Part 2") or "I must be an acrobat to talk like this and act like that" ("Acrobat"). He writes of seeking faith that connects with the nitty-gritty places in life. In the song "Mofo" he is "looking for the father of my two little girls" and "looking for the face I had before the world was made"—our ultimate goal, to become who we were made to be. This is where Paul is also heading us toward: the finish line of our redemption. Saved from the penalty of past sins, but also being continually saved from the power of sin in the present, so that we might one day be saved from the very presence of sin and restored, finding the faces we had before the foundation of the world.

That kingdom, of course, has been at the forefront of U2's music and work. Even in this song they declare belief in "the Kingdom Come," where "all the colors will bleed into one." And they are not prepared to wait until God puts it all right in heaven. They are not prepared to wait until then for poor nations to get a better trade deal. They are not prepared to wait until then for the AIDS pandemic in Africa to get a Christian response. They are not prepared to wait until then for peace in Northern Ireland. As the new millennium saw the band remove their 90s disguises and reveal their true selves once more, Bono has been crusading across the globe in an attempt to make this kingdom in which he believes so passionately more and more of a reality.

Bono told the Irish magazine *Hot Press* in late 2000: "I can't live with acquiescence. I can't make peace with myself or the world. I just can't. To me, it's like rolling over. So in doing things like Jubilee 2000, I do feel better for actually feeling that I'm getting my hands around the throat of something I care about."[4] There seems to be a fidgeting agitation at the core of Bono's soul that is set uncomfortably in motion by his belief that this cross can and should be making a difference. That difference is what he is looking for.

It is the same utter absence of acquiescence that drove Paul. His Damascus Road experience fired him forward with a passionate zeal to take the good news to the uttermost ends of the earth. There is a sense of vocation in Philippians 3:12-16: He has a fidgeting agitation to suck the marrow from this salvation that has come from God—grace.

And me? And you? Are we living with acquiescence? Have we rolled over, or are we running and crawling and scaling city walls to be with God and to bring some good news to turn the bad news of this world on its head? Where is the bad news in our communities? Where is our world out of sync with the Creator's original intentions? What would it look like to see God's will in the avenues and ghettos of our cities, on the shop floors of our factories, in the lecture halls of our institutions of learning, in the political corridors of power, in the high rise offices of commercial globalization, in the studios of art and music and film, on the pages of our literature and newspapers? This is what we are looking for. This is what we pray for. This is what we need to do—to heed the challenge from the Irish gurus to "Get up off your knees now, please!"

Various contexts in Northern Ireland

---

4   Olaf Tyaransen, "The Final Frontier," *Hot Press,* October 26, 2000

Beyond Prosperity

Jamie Parsley

Song reference: "If God Will Send His Angels"
Biblical reference: Luke 12:32–40

The other night I was talking to an old buddy from high school, Dave, who was telling me about a guy he knows, Nick, who is a very successful businessman. Nick is a member of one of those nondenominational megachurches that are so popular now, and he often goes around preaching and expounding on the Bible. One of the messages that he's fond of preaching about is the belief that God wants us all to be materially wealthy. "God wants us to have nice cars," this guy told my friend. "God wants us to have nice houses, nice clothes, trips to exotic places." But Dave isn't so sure. And so he turned to me and asked, "Is this really what God wants? Does God want us to be wealthy?"

There's a part of me that wanted to respond to Dave by saying, "Fine. If people want to look at the things in their lives as blessings from God, who am I to say anything different?" After all, I myself like nice things—whether it is food or music or fine architecture or what have you. I've fantasized about living in one of those huge houses south of town or on Eighth Street. I imagine what it would be like to have a really fast, expensive, foreign car or to fly off to Cap d'Antibes.

But the problem with this "Gospel of Prosperity," as it is called, is that it defines our faith in God by the possessions we have. That really bothers me. As pleasant as it sounds, as wonderful as it might be to believe that God is some Santa Claus in heaven whose only wish is to rain riches down upon us, the reality is this: "One's life does not consist in the abundance of possessions" (Lk. 12:15).

This is a message that seems to get lost in the version of the Gospel preached by people like Nick. His Gospel is preached by a Jesus I have a hard time recognizing. Nick's Jesus comes across as promising the goods, but not the substance. Nick's Jesus seems to believe that a well-balanced spirituality is somehow dependent upon having material goods; Nick's Jesus is some strange glitzy version of the one I have met.

There was a song by U2 a few years back that keeps going through my head as I think about this type of Jesus:

> Jesus never let me down
> You know Jesus used to show me the score
> Then they put Jesus in show business
> Now it's hard to get in the door

In the video, Bono sings this lament about the absence of God sitting in a booth in a café. And as he sits, all around him life is going on at high speed. People of all races and ages slide into the booth and carry on animated conversations. There's a fire in the dark street outside, fire trucks come, waitresses pass. And the lament for God goes on, and no one sees or notices it, even when they're sitting right next to it. They just miss the point.

In the Gospels we often find stories of Jesus meeting people who simply miss the point. The story of the rich man who meets Jesus is no exception. It portrays one person in the crowd so distracted by possessions that he's simply not seeing or hearing Jesus. He comes to Jesus because one of his brothers is not sharing an inheritance and he knows that some portion is rightfully his. Although Jesus—Savior of the world, Christ himself—is standing right there next to him, this person misses the whole point because he is too busy measuring his life in possessions. And Jesus, knowing this, says to him, "Take care, be on your guard against all kinds of greed; for one's life does not consist in the abundance of possessions!" Exclamation point. Of course, Jesus doesn't let it end there. He has to deliver the punch in that way only he can. He goes on to tell a story, a story about a rich fool who measured the value of his life only by what he had.

The point of the story is to emphasize, first and foremost, that life—our lives—and all the things we have in this life, whatever they may be, are gifts from God. These are our blessings. Yes, my dirty Pontiac Sunbird out there in the parking lot is a gift from God. It gets me where I want to go. It hasn't broken down too many times. That's a blessing in my life. So are my friends and family. None of them are perfect. None of them are millionaires or as brilliant as Einstein. But I consider them gifts from God.

Jesus is not saying that we should get rid of all our possessions. It's fine to have nice things. I like my DVD player and my computer. However, we must not define ourselves by them, nor should we obsess over them. We must not reduce life to what can be bought and sold. The young person who confronted Jesus about the inheritance could have lost the opportunity to receive the love of God that Jesus was offering in what he was saying. We too might miss out on the love God offers us in our lives when we are distracted by our possessions.

What concerns me about the "Gospel of Prosperity" that Nick preaches is that, ironic as it is, it *cheapens* Christianity. It makes the Church into some gaudy casino. And it complicates our faith more than it needs to. It says to us that the more we have, the more blessed we are. I'm sorry. That's simply not true.

What Nick—like that young man in the gospel—has failed to do is to *look*. He doesn't see where he is and who is present with him. Rather than expounding on the glories of materialism, he should, as a Christian, be looking at the loving and real presence of God in Christ in his life—a presence that comes to us no matter what possessions we have. God loves us when we're poor, too. God loves us when we have to struggle to pay the next credit card bill or the student loan or the car payment. We, too, must be careful when we define ourselves by our jobs, our possessions, or our things. We are not what we have or what we can do; we are who we are in the God who comes to us as Christ. And it is that same God who comes to us as Christ, who forgives us of everything we have

Finding The Way To The Playboy Mansion

Derek Walmsley

Song reference: "The Playboy Mansion"
Biblical reference: John 14:1–6

I love U2. I've been a fan since 1981 when I first saw them at the Greenbelt Christian Rock Festival in the south of England. That was the only time they ever played to a specifically Christian audience.

Not long after that they spoke at an invitation-only weekend for Christian musicians in the U.K. I wasn't there, but I have tapes of the event. At one point, a member of the audience asked Bono about the lyrics of his songs, complaining that they were obscure and impossible to understand. The guy clearly wanted Bono to be more explicit about his faith. Bono's reply was that he didn't "write" lyrics; he invented them as he sang at the mike in the studio.

However, in U2's later work, they paid more attention to writing carefully structured lyrics. Sixteen years later, they released an album called *Pop*, which was very different from most of what they had recorded before. The lyrics seemed more carefully structured—they continued dealing with religious themes but in a more subtle, thought-out way than in their early work.

One song mostly ignored on that album by critics and fans—and never played live—is titled "The Playboy Mansion." On the surface it's a song about stardom and fame, but the song has deeper spiritual significance for those with ears to hear.

The song begins with reflections upon the icons of our "Pop" era. It mentions Coke and Michael Jackson; it reflects on beauty and the use of surgery to maintain our youthful looks. The verses catalogue the cultural icons of our day: O.J. Simpson, McDonalds, Calvin Klein, and talk shows, money, and lottery draws. Religious imagery seeps into the lyrics as U2 suggests that talk shows have replaced confession, banks are today's cathedrals, and "Chance is a kind of religion, where you're damned for plain hard luck." Secular symbols have taken on religious roles.

So in this world, the text asks, what is salvation? Prestige? Money? And how do you attain it—just by lucking out and having your "numbers come around," being in the right place at the right time to become famous?

What am I to do?
Have I got the gifts to get me through
The gates of that mansion?

What have we got to lose?
Another push and maybe we'll be through
The gates of that mansion

The image is not surprising. After all, if fame is salvation, then heaven is a mansion—one of those palatial homes with high walls and security patrols. A Playboy mansion . . . is that what U2 is singing about?

Maybe it's more than that. Because if you've read the Bible, you've heard the word "mansion" before, in John 14, where Jesus is talking to his disciples on the night before his death. He reassures them that he is going ahead "to prepare a place" for them: "In my father's house there are many mansions." With all the other religious imagery in this song, is it possible that U2 means more than the mansions of the rich and famous? Is it possible that these lyrics have a double meaning?

As the lyrics begin to drop additional Biblical hints, it seems like Bono is singing not just about earthly mansions but also about heaven. That's confirmed by lines in the song taken from Revelation 21: "Then will there be no time of sorrow, then will there be no time for shame." He adds: "Though I can't say why, I know I've got to believe."

We know that to earn one of those earthly mansions, you need a lot of money or fame. Is it the same for the other mansion, the heavenly one? Do we earn our way to that one? Will "another push" get us through the gates?

The idea that a place in heaven is earned by the rich or even the "good" people is such a common idea—I meet it all the time in pastoral ministry. I sometimes ask people, "Do you think that you would go to heaven if you died tonight?" The answer is often, "Well, if I'm good enough."

When I ask if they are good enough, modesty usually prevents them saying anything more than "I hope so." But the Bible teaches plainly that "All have sinned and fall short of God's glory." No one reaches God's standard. It's as though the "pass mark" for heaven is way too high for anyone. Some say "I scored 500"; others say "I scored 10,000." But it doesn't matter, because the pass mark is always beyond our reach.

So how *do* we get in, if it is impossible to earn God's favor?

U2 ends this song by suggesting an answer to the question, seemingly just reminding us that in the world of fame and fortune, "it's who you know" that gets you to the top. "It's who you know that gets you through" a mansion's security gate. But in fact, there is more going on; because if we return to John 14, Jesus gives exactly that answer as well.

When Jesus prepared his disciples for his death by talking of his Father's house which contained many mansions, he declared "I am the way, the truth and the life, no one comes to the Father except by me." And at the end of that final evening with his friends, Jesus prayed a long prayer, which we are privileged to have recorded for us in John 17. As he prays to his Father, Jesus says, "Eternal life means knowing you, the one true God, and Jesus Christ whom you sent."

In other words, heaven is only accessed by a relationship with Christ. Not by good works or religious duties but by a relationship with God's son.

Wandering Sheep

Darleen Pryds

Song reference: "I Still Haven't Found What I'm Looking For"
Biblical reference: Luke 15:1–10

Losing things. It's something we all know about—that feeling of bewilderment, followed by panic and then possibly dread, when we begin searching in earnest for the keys that we can't find, the pen we were using just a minute ago, or that phone number we need. It's no wonder we turn to whatever we can.

I turn to a glow-in-the-dark statuette of St. Anthony of Padua that one of my students gave me years ago after she found her "lost" overdue term paper. St. Anthony of Padua, one of the beloved saints of the Franciscan Order, is the patron saint of lost things. I keep my statuette on my office desk. I admit it's not much to look at in the daylight, but at night, it glows. It's stunning.

For generations when Catholics lost something they'd say: "Tony, Tony turn around; something's lost and must be found!" This is the kind of stuff many of you cradle Catholics cringe at, but I love it. I especially love the fact that if people still couldn't find the object after praying to Anthony, they'd think he hadn't been working hard enough for them, so they'd turn their statue toward the wall until he got to work.

We humans are always trying to be in charge, or at least have a say in everything, even when we are in need of help. Implicit in popular piety is a recognition and acceptance of our human nature. I love these forms of popular piety because they are so *concrete;* they are so *human.*

Do they work? Maybe; maybe not.

Are they enough? No; but do they need to be?

Popular piety speaks to our immediate needs—in this case, the search for a lost object. But this immediate need reflects a deeper one we all live with—the search for faith, that fundamental human need that U2 sings about in "I Still Haven't Found What I'm Looking For."

In the Gospel reading for today, we heard a parable about a shepherd, searching for a sheep who had strayed. If God is the shepherd, we are most certainly the lost sheep.

Now, I'll be upfront and tell you that I'm a city girl who doesn't have regular contact with sheep. I had heard that sheep were dumb and stubborn, and with this information I had this reflection all worked out ahead of time in my head. Based on my limited experience with sheep, I expected to preach to you today about how sheep, like us, are dumb and obstinate. We wander away and God finds us, and we're returned to the flock.

But then one afternoon, I ran into our resident expert on sheep, Sister Eva, who set me straight on my assumptions about sheep. She pulled me aside and told me all about sheep. They're not so much dumb as persistent. They know what they need and they are persistent in seeking to get their needs met, sometimes with tragic consequences. I learned from another friend that sheep may get so thirsty that they wade into a stream and drink, only to drown from the weight of their wool laden with the very water they are drinking.

Rather like us.

Suddenly, I had a deeper appreciation of why, in this parable, Jesus used the image of sheep to characterize us. The sheep that wandered away from the flock was seeking something. It might look senseless and ridiculous to us, but there was an inner drive, an inner yearning that the sheep was trying to fill.

Indulge me for a moment to bring this into an area *I do* know about. It's like a beagle. My ten-year-old beagle Gracie, whom many of you have met, is driven by one primary thing:

her sense of smell. She'll follow her nose anywhere, including right into the middle of Hearst and Euclid, the busiest intersection around here. Stupid? No, it's her very nature. But it is her very nature that also leads her into danger, which is why I'm around to pull and tug at her and keep her safe.

Whether sheep or beagles, these animals are like us. We search for what we want most. Our very nature is to yearn for the transcendent, to yearn for the Divine. But instead of waiting for God to find us, we tend to wander, we tend to search.

But whatever we do is not enough, and may indeed even become dangerous to us if we become obsessive about it. We yearn, we seek, *and* we are utterly dependent on God to find us. We live in this tension.

Many of us in this room are members of what has been called Generation X, a generation born between 1961 and 1981. We've been called irreverent, slackers, disrespectful, unable to make commitments, and disillusioned. But in teaching a course on GenX spirituality this semester, I've learned just how intent our generation is to embrace the hard questions of faith head-on. I've learned just how much we are searching. And we find our answers in a wide variety of texts, contexts, images, and especially music.

We rarely agree on anything, I might add. The class is so spirited in its discussions and independent spirit that one student last week proclaimed, "You know, we're just really obnoxious. Whenever Darleen wants us to talk about communal worship, we talk about individual spirituality, and whenever she wants us to talk about our individual faith journeys, we insist on talking about the community. We're just obnoxious."

But there is one thing we agree on—or well, now, actually two things: that statement and the profound impact of the Irish band U2 on our spirituality. Whenever someone brings in a U2 song, the entire class sings along. The band captures our experience; they capture our searching, our yearning.

The song "I Still Haven't Found What I'm Looking For" is played at GenXer funerals and GenXer weddings. Far from being a song of disillusionment or bitterness, far from being a song declaring one's inability to make a commitment, it remains a daring proclamation of our utter dependence on faith. It expresses this tension we live with in this life: By our very nature, we seek; but we cannot find, not here on earth.

Couples who have the song played at their weddings boldly shatter all of our easy assumptions about romantic love and happily-ever-after, by using this song to declare their deeper search for God. And friends and families, preparing to bury their young people, choose this song to be sung at funerals as a reminder that the search and struggle of the deceased is finally over.

The life of our faith is not a simple one. There are popular pieties and formulaic prayers, but these are not enough. There are complex theologies, and they are not enough. We yearn for our God, and that is not enough. And, this is who we are.

> I believe in the kingdom come
> Then all the colors will bleed into one
> Bleed into one
> But yes I'm still running
>
> But I still haven't found what I'm looking for.

Franciscan School of Theology
7 November 2002

If We Were More Like Thomas

Beth Maynard

Song reference: "Tomorrow"
Biblical references: John 20:19–31, 1 Peter 1:3–9

Blessed are those who have not seen and yet have come to believe."

Do you find that comforting? I imagine that's how it's supposed to feel. When we hear that sentence at the end of the story of Thomas meeting the Risen Christ at last, John probably wants us to say to ourselves: See, even though we didn't get to meet him, the Risen Christ still likes us. Even though we weren't actually there, Jesus foresaw our existence and sent us a message: "Blessed are those who have not seen and yet have come to believe."

Now, if that's your reaction to this sentence, if it is a comfort, I am glad for you. But I just want to issue a warning that you may wish to tune me out at this point and read the catechism in the back of the Prayer Book or look up your favorite Psalm or something. Because this sentence does not make me feel all warm inside. Frankly, it annoys me, and I'm a little mad at John for putting it in.

I say that not because I dislike the verse itself, but because I think it gets used to encourage people to be satisfied with a secondhand relationship with God. People quote it as if it means that God was available long ago when Jesus was on earth, and well, even though we missed all the fun, we should be satisfied with just hearing about the things Jesus did and believing the testimony that they happened.

So what do you mean, you don't find that a big comfort? It says you should right here: "Blessed are those who have not seen and yet have come to believe."

Now, before we go any further, I'm not saying that there is anything wrong, in general, with believing based on somebody's testimony. You know, we have some compelling external authorities in the Christian faith. The two big ones are even hinted at in this passage.

There is Tradition: the testimony of the disciples to whom Jesus appeared. "We have seen the Lord." That is what the voice of Tradition sounds like. "We believe in One God." That corporate memory of the church is one of the external authorities that give us grounds for believing.

And then the other one, Scripture, is referred to right at the end: "These [signs] are written so that you may come to believe that Jesus is the Messiah . . . and that through believing you may have life in his name." The writer looks straight at the reader for a second there, reminding us why we have a Bible in the first place.

So yes, we Christians do believe things based on the testimony of external authorities. And that's fine, as long as the authorities are reliable—which I believe they are. But respecting Scripture and Tradition is not a substitute for our own questioning, our own seeing, our own direct approach to God.

In fact, both Scripture and Tradition point the way to something more, something quite marvelous—and that goes not just for the first disciples who saw Jesus in the flesh, but for us as well. In the Gospel of Matthew, Jesus makes that promise that is so familiar: "For where two or three are gathered in my name, I am there among them." And the author of the letter to the Hebrews insists that things have not changed: "Jesus Christ is the same yesterday and today, and forever." Even this morning, the language from 1 Peter was glowing: "A new birth into a living hope," it promised, "an indescribable and glorious joy."

If that is truly what's available, then let's have it. I don't want anybody to try and satisfy me with a platitude, an old book, or a consolation prize. I know this phrase is required

IRS legalese, but I'd even rather you didn't send me receipts for donations that tell me all I'm getting from this church is "intangible religious benefits." I don't want intangible religious benefits; I want what was advertised.

Thomas did too. Some people fault him for that. They read him as a cynic and a debunker. I read him as a person with a passion for truth. Sure, it would have been comforting to believe that Jesus was alive, but seriously, can you imagine anything more fantastically improbable? Thomas wasn't willing to sit there in that upper room and take comfort in an easy platitude or a secondhand reassurance. If he was going to be comforted, it would have to be by reality.

I love that attitude in Thomas. I love it wherever I find it, but one example that has always especially moved me is in a very early song by the rock group U2. The song is simply called "Tomorrow." Its narrator seems to be in a similar situation to Thomas, and like Thomas, he is asking a lot of questions and flatly refusing to take the easy way out.

For the initial few minutes, the whole ambiance is so atmospheric and misty that it's difficult to tell what's going on. The first thing we hear is the chorus, a question repeated over and over: "Won't you come back tomorrow?" As we move into the verses, we begin to suspect that we are shut in a room somewhere, surrounded by family grieving a recent death. We begin to suspect that we are, in fact, just where the ten apostles, minus Thomas and Judas, were at the beginning of today's Gospel—behind locked doors, staring at each other numbly and muttering, "He's gone. Now what are we going to do?"

The song goes on to tell us, "Somebody's knocking at the door. There's a black car parked by the side of the road." That can't be good. This is going to hurt, isn't it? And then someone offers a tempting piece of advice: "Don't go to the door."

How often have we heard that suggestion? Turn your head, put on blinders, have a beer. Believe whatever works for you, whatever dulls the pain. Comfort yourself with some platitudes: It was probably for the best. When reality comes knocking, just don't go to the door.

But the narrator refuses to hide. He vows, "I'm going out there!" My guess is that this song draws on U2's frontman and drummer both having lost their mothers in their teens, so when I listen to that moment of bravado, I usually picture a young man. But I also picture Thomas behind today's Gospel's locked doors, or I picture myself. "I'm going out there." Whatever it is, I want to see it face to face. I don't care if it hurts. "I'm going out."

So, against everyone's advice, the narrator nervously heads for that door, still asking questions. The song hints that what he really wants to know is not just if he will see his mother again, but if there is any hope in a world where death is irrevocable. He wonders about Jesus' death: "Who tore the curtain and who was it for?" And about the notion that Jesus might have some power over pain: "Who healed the wounds? Who heals the scars?"

Surrounded by questions, the singer tries to bolster his own courage: "Open the door," he tells himself, and maybe us too: "Open the door." And it's hard not to wonder if this is another inquisitive glance at Jesus, quoting the classic line from the King James translation of Revelation 3: "Behold, I stand at the door, and knock: if any man hear my voice, and open the door, I will come in to him."

The chorus has been repeating throughout: "Won't you come back tomorrow? Will you be back tomorrow?" And, as often happens to pronouns in U2 songs, that "you" has grown more spacious since we first heard it. All those questions and allusions have made room in it for more than just a single person the singer has lost. That "you" is big enough now for whatever we'll encounter when the door swings open.

I can see him—Thomas, the singer—with his hand on the knob. All it takes is one last step.

And as he opens the door onto reality, the song—his world—is transformed. It's an extraordinary moment. We aren't told Who is standing there, but we can guess. The narrator is overcome, incoherent with adoration. He struggles to speak: "I want . . . I really . . . I, I want . . ." Under this stammering, the music begins to tremble and build, and then he finally gets it out: "I want You! I want You to be back tomorrow!" And the drums and guitar kick in and the entire thing just explodes.

The same experience happens to Thomas. He can only manage five words, and I'm sure he stammered as well: "My Lord and my God!" And with him, we soar up into an exaltation so ecstatic that even many U2 fans think the end of this song is just too far over the top. Of course, I guess some people think Thomas' "my Lord and my God" is kind of over the top, too.

But I can't blame U2 for their youthful enthusiasm any more than I can blame Thomas for his ecstatic, groundbreaking confession. Because both of them are trying to express something literally ineffable: The firsthand discovery of a kind of knowledge that is self-authenticating, and instantaneous, and indistinguishable from love. The firsthand experience of Someone to whom you can only say: I want You. My Lord and my God.

And see, that's where honest doubt gets us. If the narrator of "Tomorrow" hadn't gone to the door, we would never have heard the thrilling finale. If Thomas had bowed to peer pressure and grudgingly convinced himself that believing secondhand was enough for him, he would never have met the Risen Lord. If he had not pushed his assumptions and fears to the point where they ran up against God himself, we would have lost his unique witness to the deity of Christ.

When we doubt, when we want to get clearer or understand better, when we refuse to call off our own spiritual search just because someone else found God, that is a good sign, not a bad one. If we are honest skeptics, seeking reality and confronting the hard questions, that kind of doubt will bring us closer to God.

It is true that we have not seen as the apostles saw. But if we have doubted as Thomas did, we may know already that following our questions can lead straight to encountering Jesus alive. And encountering Jesus alive is where the power is.

It's been 2000 years, and so many of us who call ourselves Christians still haven't doubted enough, asked enough. We still haven't gone to the door. We've barely begun to tap the power of the Resurrection to transform ourselves and our world.

A Buddhist monk once said to an Episcopal priest, "You Christians have something absolutely wonderful. But I don't think you've got the slightest idea what it is."

Well, what is it? If we were more like Thomas, I bet we'd find out.

Trinity Church
Huntington, West Virginia
Easter 2, Year A, 1996

part **5**

elevation

The body experiences so much glory in that of the soul that in its own way it magnifies God, feeling in its bones something similar to what David declares: All my bones shall say: God, who is like to you? (Ps. 35:10). And because everything that can be said of this unction is less than what it is, it is sufficient to say in reference to both the bodily and the spiritual experience, "That tastes of eternal life."

— St. John of the Cross, *Commentary on The Living Flame of Love* [1]

"I want you." It's one of the most terrifying and most exciting, the strongest and most vulnerable phrases I know. It's something said in either a whisper or an ecstatic cry, and it asks as much as it declares. It evokes touching skin; hovering breath; limbs entwining. The coming together of body to body, of spirit to flesh.

Consummation of the cry "I want you," the union of two becoming one, may be the most powerful image we have of union with God, with Love. Desire is primal and universal.

Those who deny its power, who teach shame and disdain of the body and its hunger for union, are only fleeing from the naked vulnerability of desire, and from the way Jesus showed as the fullest expression of God's self-giving love: a human being who needs a community of flesh and spirit, who hungers and thirsts for companionship and comfort and union as much as for food and water and air.

Incarnation, becoming flesh and being flesh, is not descent. Here, hovering over the hips, the thighs, the chest, the neck, the lips, the eyes, knowing my need for one who needs me, my love of one who loves me, my honor and adoration of one who honors and adores me, I come closer to knowing what it means to be human in God's image. Here, in breath on skin and breath in breath, in the love and peace and gentleness and yes, in the desire—in the Yes—is the Spirit. When my love for you gives you power and nourishment to be who you most truly are, your mouth tastes of eternal life. Elevate me; let me lift you as my hunger for you lifts me.

We should say grace in the marriage bed, bless the hunger and the filling and the hungering again. All we have known and experienced and loved we have done in and through these bodies, these spiritual gifts of flesh. The messianic banquet is a wedding feast, where all—those called to singleness who have hungered to love the world, those in fleshly spiritual unions with another human being, those grieving the loss of one much-loved—will know the union in whose image all life-giving unions are made. Now, our love is veiled, and we ask for and offer promises and trinkets. Then, our bones, our skin and flesh, our tongues, and our souls will offer with abandon what God offers us now: I want you. All I want is you.

Sarah Dylan Breuer

---

1 *The Collected Works of St. John of the Cross*, trans. Kieran Kavanaugh, ocd and Otilio Rodriguez, ocd (Washington, D.C.: ICS Publications, 1979), 603.

The Coming of Love

Julie Bogart

Song reference: "When Love Comes to Town"
Biblical reference: John 15:12

Most of us can remember a day love broke into our lives. Real love. A friend listened to you pour out your story of pain and didn't interrupt or give you advice. Your father forgave you when you crashed his car. Money appeared in an envelope from an anonymous source right at Christmas after you lost your job. A song's lyrics were so powerful and true that you wept and felt less alone. Take a moment to think of that time when you felt beyond repair, beyond reach, beyond return—and love broke in.

Most of the time when Christians talk about love, we use abstractions. We remind each other that love forgives our sins through Christ, that God loves and accepts us just the way we are. Some people go so far as to say that you won't always feel loved, but you ought to just believe you are loved. But those beliefs don't produce the kind of life-change we long for. We want to feel loved, not be told we are loved. We want to know we are accepted, not simply hope we are accepted.

U2's lead singer and lyricist Bono wrote a song called "When Love Comes to Town" that I'd like to use as a way of reflecting on the transforming power of love. We'll take the following biblical passage as a reference point: "This is my commandment, that you love one another as I have loved you" (Jn. 15:12). Often preachers will focus on the first half of this passage: We are to love one another. Today I'd like to focus on the second half: "I have loved you."

"When Love Comes to Town" focuses on the power of "I love you" when it comes in a form that we recognize and can experience—love that is personalized, tailor-made, to be experienced, not simply believed.

The lyrics begin by rooting us in images of ordinary people—a sailor lost at sea, a fighter who picks fights, lovers who get pleasure without commitment. All of us in our day-to-day lives are liars, lost, justly accused of the things we've said and done. We fail to appreciate our impact on others; we let them down. Over time, we become numb to living and numb to the ways we damage others. Love can't come if we fail to see that we are in need of a savior, in need of transformation.

Self-awareness comes right before we see that love is being offered to us. Something catalyzes the change, the self-analysis, and the personal reflection. Before love can meet our needs, we have to see our need. And we usually do. We get low enough, or we are sick of ourselves enough, or we feel lost or broken or dirty. That awareness opens the way for love to come in.

There is a catalyzing event that moves us to "jump that train" of love. In this song, self-awareness comes through the surprising vehicle of a screaming guitar: "I ran into a juke joint when I heard a guitar scream . . . as the music played I saw my life turn around." Right before love comes to town, our lives flash before our eyes. There is a moment in which things become clear and we have a choice: receive and be changed, or turn away. We get to look again, to see what we missed before, to realize our need. Notice that the music played as this individual saw his life turn around. That's the beginning of the transformation. Music is the gateway here. Seeing yourself accurately opens the door for love to come in:

When I woke up I was sleeping on the street
I felt the world was dancing
And I was dirt beneath their feet
When I looked up I saw the Devil looking down
But my Lord He played guitar the day love came
to town

What is the net result in our own lives of being lost, being a liar, picking fights, taking affection and intimacy from someone to whom we are not committed? The realization of failure. It leaves us low, needing a lift. Love is the impossible moment of acceptance when we feel unworthy, like "dirt beneath their feet" with a laughing devil winning his game at our expense. We feel like dirt when we lead lives that abuse other people, that take for granted goodness elsewhere, when we mean to rip off or deceive. All of us have let people down, have abandoned promises, have offered love insincerely. It's an inevitable part of being human:

I was there when they crucified my Lord
I held the scabbard when the soldier drew his sword
I threw the dice when they pierced his side

Hopeless! Even in our apparent passivity we are complicit in evil. We hold the scabbard, we throw the dice, we stand by and watch. But what stops this torrent of inevitability? Love. That's what does it! "But I've seen love conquer the great divide." Right in the moment of our greatest betrayals, our most appalling weaknesses, our self-deception and inability to turn anything around, love comes to town, love conquers the great divide:

When love comes to town
I want to jump that train
When love comes to town
I want to catch that flame

Love is an overused word. We can love our fellow man; we can love chocolate ice cream. Here, love is about the power of transformation. For the narrator here, love came in a song. It came in the form of a screaming guitar. His Lord played guitar the day love came to town, turning music into a gateway for love, the vehicle of soul awakening. We all have gateways for love. What are yours? The arts? The wonder of the stars and planets? Do you find that incomprehensible sense of peace and acceptance taking a hike in the mountains, standing by an ocean? Do you connect to others like yourself through the Internet and other relationships?

Love opens the soul to see what it didn't see before. It offers us a way out of the inevitabilities of life. It says, "Hop that train!" Love ignites. It lets us leave behind what we did before love came to town. When love comes, it sneaks up and breaks in and conquers. Love is the ultimate stealth attack. So what is this love that does it all? How do we get it? Can we book a flight, buy a ticket, bring a candle, strike a match to help it? I don't think so. Love comes unexpectedly, and when it comes, it comes in a way that you can grab hold.

Love comes as inevitably as death. It is the death of self-ishness and the resurrection of hope. It doesn't just soothe or appease. It conquers. It gets all the way down inside of us and opens a door. It offers a ride; it ignites a flame. Love does it all. Not love in the abstract, but love that each person recognizes and experiences. You know when you've been loved. You don't have to write sermons about it, you don't have to convince yourself of love. Love conquers—it takes back territory that was unloved and marks it.

Love comes, but it comes in a different form for each person. The author of love can play screaming guitar, if that's what you need. The author of love can be the train engineer, the lit candle, the friend who forgives you. Love reaches out to us personally if we have the ears to hear and the eyes to see. The author of love takes the form that will reach you. What brings that light and hope to you? How did love come to your town?

What might you do when love comes to town? First, open your life to love. Receive it from whatever source offers it. Don't judge the offering, receive it in the name of God. How is love breaking into your life right this moment—through music? Art? Friends? A second chance? Rehab? Internet support groups? Poetry? Nature? The author of love is tailor-making a package that will reach you where you are.

Second, if you are already one who has "jumped that train," has "caught that flame," it's time to be that source of love to those the world is dancin' on. How is that done? Do the thing that drives you to passionate awareness of love. Do it openly—that guitar *screamed!* Give love away—even to the ones who are holding the scabbard and throwing the dice. Be the messenger when love comes to town.

December 2002

A Wedding Sermon for Nathan and Sandie

Steven Garber

Song reference: "Grace"
Biblical reference: John 4:1–26

Grace. . .
takes the blame
covers the shame
makes beauty out of ugly things

A few weeks ago my son Jonathan and I went to the U2 concert in Baltimore with one of my closest friends, Mark. I first met Mark here in Pittsburgh years ago when he was working hard to understand the nature of Christian political responsibility. We used to eat breakfast at the Bagel Nosh, wondering together about the meaning of the Lordship of Christ for the public square in an increasingly pluralist society. Years later, like us, he moved with his family to Washington, DC, choosing a house near ours, and he has become one of the most thoughtful, faithful lovers of

God on Capitol Hill, as he leads other leaders in reflecting on the gospel of the kingdom and its implications for political life.

Of many stories, one is important here. A year ago, as chief of staff for the chiefs of staff in the Senate, Mark hosted Bono for a conversation about Jubilee. Bono had come to Washington to walk the corridors of the Capitol asking that the world be set right, economically, socially, politically—in the name of Jubilee.

A small request, really.

For some twenty years now, U2 has been the most important musical group in the world. Their politically and theologically rich artistic vision, fueled by unbounded creativity and passion, has given them a truly global audience—people hang on their words. My friend Mark began to do so himself as an undergraduate at Penn State in the early 1980s.

Bono came to Washington with sunglasses and a smile, but he was completely serious too, wondering aloud about the political possibilities of grace. Because, of course, it is grace that is at the very heart of the Jubilee vision. Because, of course, it is grace that "takes the blame, covers the shame, makes beauty out of ugly things" in the most personal strains of human life and in the most public of struggles. From friendships and families in which the brokenness of the world is felt so painfully, all the way through to political and economic relationships between nations that have become distorted and skewed, across the spectrum of human responsibilities and relationships, it is the Jubilee vision of grace incarnate that alone—*alone*—has the possibility of setting the world right.

But it is so, so hard to see it happen. The world, the flesh, and the devil conspire against that possibility, and we grieve and groan, longing for our lives and our world to be made right. Don't we? As hard as it is, though, we live in faith and hope and love, believing that it is true, that grace—always and everywhere—"takes the blame, covers the shame, makes beauty out of ugly things." Believing that to be true, as the family and friends of Sandie and Nathan, we have come together to grace you, and to call you to a life of grace—yes, to a Jubilee vision—as you promise faithful love one to the other, before us, and more importantly, before the face of God.

Dear ones, I want to set before you this day what is the most difficult challenge facing us as we try to live lives of grace. In fact, I believe it is the most difficult challenge that human beings face. No task that we take up as sons of Adam and daughters of Eve is more perplexing than the problem we encounter in trying to know and to love at the very same time. To know you *and* to love you? *Please.*

Mostly, we don't. We find it too hard, too burdensome, too costly. How is it possible to really know someone, with their fragility and foibles, with their sinful selfishness, and to love them, too? Mostly, we don't. This is true across human experience, from the most individual clay-footedness to the most institutional complexities. When we really know, that is, see someone as he or she really is, see something as it really is, we walk away—sometimes with sadness, often with cynicism. And we say, "*Now* I know!"

But do we really? Is that what it means to know? To see, and become cynical? To hear, and become hard? The world does it that way, time and time and time again. I see it in Washington, year in, year out. People come from all over the world, eager and motivated to take up public service— Potomac fever, we call it—and then months, maybe years later, finding that the political, economic, and social worlds are badly broken, walk away, saying to all who will hear, "*Now* I know!"

But is that what it means to know? Not for a moment. For people whose visions and virtues are shaped by Scripture, to know means to love.

For Hebrew people, reflecting upon and dwelling within the worldview which grew out of the covenant, to *know* meant to *care*. Chapter after chapter, century after century, there is an integral relationship between knowing and caring. Poignantly, the very first use of the verb "to know" in the Bible comes to us in a commentary on the meaning of marriage. Adam knew Eve his wife. In commitment and intimacy, Adam knew Eve his wife. In her glory and her shame, Adam knew and loved Eve his wife (Gen. 4:1). But "to know" comes to us in its most truthful expression in God's knowing of his people. "I have seen the misery of my people in Egypt . . . and I care about them" (cf. Ex. 3:7). We say "I care," but the Hebrew is literally "I know." Theologically and etymologically, *to care* is written into the very verb *to know*.

The Proverbs offer a window into this dynamic understanding of knowing as caring: "The righteous care about justice for the poor . . . the wicked have no such concern" (Prov.
29:7, NIV). For the prophets, if you know, you care; if you
don't care, then you don't know. To offer faithful love to God
and the world was seen as the very same as true knowledge of
God. "Hear the word of the Lord, you Israelites, because the
Lord has a charge to bring against you who live in the land:
'There is no faithfulness, no love, no knowledge of God in the
land. There is only cursing, lying, and murder, stealing and
adultery . . . because of this the land mourns, and those who
live in it waste away'" (cf. Hos. 4:1–3).

Then, wonder of wonders, comes a day when this theological vision becomes embodied. The Word becomes flesh, and
lives for awhile among us. In the second person of the Trinity,
God incarnates the truth that to know is to care, to know is
to love. And perhaps nowhere do we see that more clearly
than in the story of Jesus and the Samaritan woman (Jn. 4).
It is a story of human longing, of the desire to be known *and*
loved at the same time. Sad and honest, it is a story of how
horribly hard it is to give grace and to find grace, to love in
the ruins of a broken world.

Jesus begins by purposefully seeking out a woman who is
lost in the cosmos. Water—would you like a drink of water?
In the heart and mind of Jesus that water becomes a water
which satisfies every thirst: for commitment and intimacy, to
know and love, to be known and loved, here and tomorrow,
in this life and the next.

The Samaritan woman is a woman with seemingly
unquenchable thirsts, apparently unquenchable longings.
And they have not been satisfied, though she has tried, again
and again and again. With what can only be called amazing
grace, Jesus offers her living water, and she responds, "I want
that, please!"

Omniscient, all-wise, God of love and truth, Jesus asks her
about her history of husbands. Daughter of Eve that she is,
image-bearer of God that she is, she is *known*—one more time,
by one more man. What might it have felt like to be so fully
known? I imagine the woman felt very vulnerable. It is, of
course, in our sexual and relational stumbling that we are
most afraid of being known. We are more fragile, more frail
there than anywhere.

But the text tells us a different tale than we might imagine from our own experience. In her encounter with Jesus, the Samaritan woman felt deeply, profoundly loved in the act of being known. She had been known by many men but loved by none. And yet, now she is known *and* loved, at the very same time. Wonder of wonders.

Nathan and Sandie, I remember the first year of my marriage (yes, there were fireworks as love flourished between us—thanks be to God!). But there were also places of pain. Each and every time, the grieving and groaning came from a dissonance between knowing and loving. If there was one question I asked time and again that first year, it was this: Do you still love me; can you still love me; now that you know me, is it possible to love me?

The wonderful writer Wendell Berry helps all of us understand how it is we can know and love at the same time. He explores this theme on almost every page he writes. In an essay titled "Word and Flesh," he says:

> Love is never abstract. . . . Love is not, by its own desire, heroic. It is heroic only when compelled to be. It exists by its willingness to be anonymous, humble, and unrewarded.
>
> The older love becomes, the more clearly it understands its involvement in partiality, imperfection, suffering, and mortality. Even so, it longs for incarnation.[2]

In another essay, he remembers his pilgrimage of leaving his home and his family's farm in Kentucky, going off to the university, finding a job teaching writing in New York City, and thinking, "I have arrived!" But then he begins to wonder again about Kentucky, eventually deciding to return home to teach and write and farm. As he put it, "This place was my 'subject matter.'" As the years went by, though, he began to see and hear differently. He began to *know* differently.

> I began to live in my subject, and to learn that living in one's subject is not at all the same as "having" a sub-

---

2 Wendell Berry, "Word and Flesh," in *What Are People For?* (San Francisco: North Point Press, 1990), 200.

ject. . . . One's relation to one's subject ceases to be merely emotional or esthetical, or even merely critical, and becomes problematical, practical, and responsible as well. Because it must. It is like marrying your sweetheart.[3]

From conversations we have had, this year and over the years, you know that I believe that marriage is a long friendship. It is not, nor can it ever be, a long date. We do not fall in love and then get married. We get married, and then learn what love requires. Friendships, like all human relationships, face the challenge we have been reflecting upon: Can we know and love, can one be known and be loved, at the same time? Friendship within marriage, when there is flourishing for husbands and for wives, is marked by grace, by the decision to give grace. The choice to give grace, the act of giving grace, is rooted in the reality that to know means to love.

As Jonathan and I walked out of the concert several weeks ago, completely astounded by the musicality, by the sacramental quality, of U2's performance that night, we heard these words wafting through the arena.

Grace. . .

> takes the blame
> covers the shame
> makes beauty out of ugly things.

As true as those words were for the thousands who gathered that night to sing the songs of Zion, plastic cups of beer high overhead, they are true for all of us here this day. And to you, Sandie and Nathan, they are true for you. They are words of life, for life—not of death, for death. May they be life, may they bring life to you, dear, dear friends, as you take up the graces and glories, as well as the responsibilities and routines of becoming husband and wife.

Shadyside Presbyterian Church
Pittsburgh, Pennsylvania
17 November 2001

---

3 Wendell Berry, "The Making of a Marginal Farm," in *Recollected Essays 1965–1980* (San Francisco: North Point Press, 1981), 337.

The Voice You Find May Be Your Own

Anna Carter Florence

Song reference: "I Still Haven't Found What I'm Looking For"
Biblical reference: Mark 14:1–9

Part of my job, when I was a minister for youth and young adults, was to keep up with popular culture, especially music. Now that my husband and I live at a boarding school and run a dorm of ninth-grade boys, I think that whether I like it or not, the music keeps up with me, mostly as it comes pounding through the floor. Our fourteen-year-old boys don't talk a lot, at least not to us. They talk through their stereos. And they talk through the volume control on their stereos. So the music is important. Usually I can tell what kind of day someone's had by what music he's listening to—and how loud it is. Sometimes I understand or even like what I hear; sometimes I don't. Sometimes I really, really miss the point—which is occasionally to my credit. But what always interests me is to hear these guys playing music that I know and love, music that speaks to me, too, and even for me, just as it speaks for them.

I had one of those music moments a few weeks ago when I passed the room of two of our most co-operationally challenged students. They were listening to *The Joshua Tree* by U2, the Irish rock band. If you are not familiar with this group, you need to know that U2 is widely regarded as one of the most talented and political bands of the last decade. They also speak openly about the impact of their Christian faith on their music, which is a rare thing for a group that is often featured on MTV.

U2 is big with everyone from the critics down, and they are very big with me. And here were two of our toughest cases, cranking up the volume on a song that is so beautiful that it has become a kind of anthem. The lyrics go like this:

> I believe in the Kingdom Come
> when all the colors will bleed into one,
> but yes I'm still running.
> You broke the bonds,
> You loosed the chains,
> You carried the cross and my shame;
> you know I believe it.
> But I still haven't found what I'm looking for.

Whether you are a boy on the brink of adulthood or a mother with small children, on some days, that about sums it up: "I believe, but I still haven't found what I'm looking for." For a moment, those kids and I moved beyond the discipline and whining and banter that usually mark our exchanges, to find that we had the same voice, and it felt great.

There is a basic truth here, beneath the youthful romance. Life is a gift, not a picnic, and we all know it. But along the way, there are moments we can touch, music we can feel, lyrics we can relate to, people we can admire who touch chords deep within us and give us moments of recognition. One moment, we are singing the refrain, "I still haven't found what I'm looking for"; the next, we discover, in the midst of our searching, that we have found a new voice. And surprise! The voice we find may be our own.

Such a moment could start with a song—maybe it probes an emotion buried so deep that you had forgotten it was there. It could start with a teacher—maybe she opens a door to a whole new world you hadn't even imagined. It could start with a story—maybe it helps you to claim something that you didn't think you could ever claim.

Such a moment could start with Jesus.

The woman with the alabaster jar has created quite a stir among biblical scholars. Matthew, Mark, Luke, and John tell their own versions, each a little different. They agree on what the *disciples* did, which was to attack the woman, and on what *Jesus* did, which was to defend her. But they can't agree on what the *woman* did!

Who was she? Was she an honorable member of society, or a sinner? Was she Mary, the sister of Lazarus, or Mary Magdalene, who had seven demons, or a woman whose name has been lost? Did she interrupt the meal, or was the dinner at her house? Was the ointment worth two hundred silver pieces or three hundred, and was she wealthy enough to afford it or not? Did she anoint his head, as one would do for a king, or his feet, as one would do for a corpse? Did her tears fall on his feet, or was she dry-eyed? And most important—did she let her hair down, which would have been a scandalous act, not unlike her taking off her shirt in public, or did she not?

Scholars and preachers get very worked up about these sorts of ambiguities, probably because it's our job to do that, but traditional interpretations have generally agreed on one thing: This story functions as a prefiguration of Jesus' death and messiahship. The woman is secondary. Who she was and what she did and what she believed are narrative details that can be, and in fact have been, eclipsed by the big picture.

To which I say, balderdash!

Something happens to us on the way from childhood to adulthood. We all start out as cheeky babies with full-blown lungs, spunky four-year-olds with opinions about everything, confident grade-schoolers who can take on the world, and then—wham!—adolescence hits us square in the face. It isn't just that the world is bigger and scarier than before. It isn't just that we have to trade our cheek and spunk for things like responsibility and accountability. It's the gender issues that get out of control. No matter who we are or in what time or context we live, the day comes when we are all informed that it is time to stop playing and to start behaving like real women, real men, and if we aren't sure what that means, we can get in buckets of trouble. Our bodies chip in their own two cents by going hormonally haywire, just to cement the fact that something has changed irrevocably. From now on, we cannot simply be human beings; we must be identifiable as *feminine* human beings, *masculine* human beings.

I think the voice is the first thing to go. I see it in our silent boys, who communicate via compact disc, but I see it in the girls, too, who will talk freely among themselves, but only haltingly and deferentially when in mixed-gender groups and in the classroom. And while I am pretty sure our boys will eventually decide that being masculine means speaking up and stating their opinions, I am not at all sure the girls will decide that being feminine means the same thing.

Presumably you and I are communicating through something more than stereos these days. But the voice is a tricky thing; it comes and goes, all our lives. Whenever we are scared to say what we really think, or to stand up for what we really believe, or to step outside the bounds of what it means to be identifiably feminine or masculine, something catches in the throat. We lose our voice, our sense of who we are in relation to God and the world. As Nancy Ramsay puts it, we lose our relational competence. It can happen to anyone, and it hurts.

Maybe, just maybe, this was true for the woman with the alabaster jar. She wasn't a literary device on the way to a coronation. She was a person who had just had an encounter with the living God! It made her engage in some pretty out-of-bounds behavior, considering she was a feminine person, and the dangerous question is *Why?* Why would a woman perform this extravagant, sensual, absolutely forbidden act in front of a crowd of disapproving men? Whether she was some nameless female falling apart at the seams, or whether she was Mary, the very "together," dignified, and intelligent sister of Lazarus, what could she possibly gain from it? Remember, these were not her peers. They could have had her thrown out of the house, even beaten her, for creating such a scandal. As it was, they settled for merely humiliating her, because we all know you can't poke a hole in the dike of femininity without flooding the whole human landscape.

I think that what happened was very simple. Something in Mary, or whoever she was, responded to something about Jesus, and she found her voice. Maybe it was the way he really listened to her, even though she was only a woman. Maybe it was how he lived his life, honestly, simply, courageously, empathically. Maybe it was how he didn't care what others said or thought about him. Maybe it was the fact that he believed in the power of God to give life, believed it so much that it was real. Hadn't he raised Mary's brother Lazarus from the dead? It was all these things—and more. It was the way this woman felt when she was with Jesus: sure of herself, sure of God, sure of the life around her and within her. She found her voice again, and the sound of it was so clear and so true that she did the most outrageous, glorious thing she could think of to show Jesus that she understood who he was, why he was, and what he was asking of her and everyone else. *She got it!* And he loved her for it.

Maybe there have been times in your life when you've said, *"Wait! I get it!"* Maybe you have been the woman with the alabaster jar. You may have spoken up at a time when your friends warned you it was better just to keep quiet. You may have chosen the career you really wanted and thought you were good at—not to mention *called* to, even though your parents didn't approve. You may have started a relationship when everyone predicted the worst, or you may have ended one when everyone thought you were crazy to break it off. You may have decided to come out to your friends or your family or your church and tell them that you're gay or lesbian, even though it can be costly to be so honest.

It may have felt outrageous at the time. It may not have been very feminine or very masculine of you, but maybe it was the truest, clearest thing you ever did. Maybe the voice you found was your own.

We need to concede that the dinner guests do have a point about one thing. In real life, people do not go and pour twenty thousand dollars' worth of pure gold all over somebody's feet when a hundred starving children could be fed and clothed with the same money. That is called waste—even sin— and I think I would have been right in there on my high horse about it. But where we only see the impractical, Jesus sees the sacred. "Leave her alone," he tells us. "She has done a beautiful thing to me. You will always have the poor. You will always have injustice on this earth because you cannot imagine anything else, and as long as it lurks among us it is your responsibility to do something about it with your own gifts, not hers. *Her* gift is a beautiful thing. If you had eyes to see what she sees and ears to hear what she hears about who I am and what is to come, you would know this. If you had the guts to imagine what this world could be, you would be down on your knees."

Toni Morrison's novel *Beloved* is set in Ohio, just after the Civil War. The characters are a group of former slaves who are trying, despite the most unspeakable suffering, to claim their new lives and their own voice. They need help and they need healing, and for that they turn to their spiritual leader, an old woman named Baby Suggs. Here is the scene:

> When warm weather came, Baby Suggs, holy, followed by every black man, woman and child who could make it through, took her great heart to the Clearing. . . . She did not tell them to clean up their lives or to go and sin no more. She did not tell them they were the blessed of the earth, its inheriting meek or its glory-bound pure. She told them that the only grace they could have was the grace they could imagine. That if they could not see it, they would not have it.[4]

It is a beautiful thing to find your own voice. It gives you the grace to imagine that things can be better, that *we* can be better. It is a beautiful thing, a beautiful gift.

May you believe in the kingdom come
when all the colors will bleed into one, bleed into one.
May you believe that he broke the bonds,
loosed the chains,
carried the cross and all your shame, all your shame.
May you find what you're looking for. Amen.

Princeton Theological Seminary
Women in Church and Ministry Conference
5 March 1996

Originally published in the Princeton Seminary Bulletin, vol. 17 no. 2, 1996, p. 211–215. Reprinted with permission and minor changes by the author.

---

4 Toni Morrison, *Beloved* (New York: Alfred A. Knopf, 1987), 87–88.

Love's Dim Reflection

Shawnthea Monroe-Mueller

Song reference: "One"
Biblical reference: 1 Corinthians 13

In the course of planning a wedding, a couple asked if the U2 song "One" could be played during the ceremony. Reading the stony look on my face, the bride quickly added, "It's a song about love."

I've conducted enough weddings in my time that I'm no longer upset by special requests or outrageous customs. I no longer flinch when the bride enters the sanctuary decked out in a strapless cocktail dress, shoulders dusted with glitter. Wedding coordinators who suggest the baptismal font would look "more festive" draped with tulle have no power over me. Couples who believe, in spite of convincing evidence to the contrary, that pre-verbal toddlers make excellent ring bearers, have my sympathy, not my scorn. As long as the ceremony retains the appropriate spirit of worship and reverence, I believe in giving the bride and groom ample room to express themselves on their special day. But playing "One" during the ceremony tested my liberal limits.

True, it is a song about love, but not the sort of love one generally celebrates at weddings. It begins:

Is it getting better,
Or do you feel the same?
Will it make it easier on you
Now you got someone to blame

Hardly a modern version of "O Perfect Love," it's more like the soundtrack for a divorce than a wedding. The lead singer, Bono, appears to have penned an ode to a dysfunctional relationship. The lover has had enough. The relationship is on the rocks and the love the couple once shared has become twisted and deformed:

You say love is a temple
Love a higher law.
You ask me to enter
And then you make me crawl
And I can't be holding on
To what you got
When all you got is hurt.

These lyrics stand in sharp contrast to the apostle Paul's thoughts on love from 1 Corinthians 13, by far the most popular text for wedding services. Paul writes: "Love is patient; love is kind; love is not envious or boastful or arrogant or rude. It does not insist on its own way; it is not irritable or resentful; it does not rejoice in wrongdoing, but rejoices in the truth. It bears all things, believes all things, hopes all things, endures all things. Love never ends" (1 Cor. 13: 4–8).

Years ago, I read this passage to a confirmation class and one young woman perked up and said, "I recognize that! My dad read it at his second wedding." The irony was lost on all but me. The sad truth is that we live in an age when fully half of all marriages end in divorce. Of the couples who stay together, how many have achieved the kind of perfect love of which Paul writes? Very few, I'd imagine. Even the best relationships experience times of conflict, often over the smallest issues.

My parents, who've been happily married for 38 years, have had some major arguments. One epic battle was over how to dust book shelves. My mother, being a perfectionist, believes that all the books must be removed from the shelf for it to be properly dusted. My father, being my father, believes that pushing the books back, dusting the exposed shelf and then pulling the books forward is sufficient effort. So much for love not insisting on its own way. My parents are not atypical. Couples seeking counseling often discover the source of their trouble is the day to day issues—money, childcare, and housework.

It seems rather cynical, then, if not hypocritical, to speak of perfect love and lifelong commitment when experience and statistics indicate we are capable of neither. The reality of marriage is more like "One" than 1 Corinthians 13. Perhaps Bono has a better understanding of human love than Paul had.

Of course, Paul wasn't writing about love between a man and a woman. Scholars are quick to point out that the thirteenth chapter of 1 Corinthians is not Paul's advice to newlyweds. Rather, it is a development of his discourse on the nature and character of true Christian community. Real Christian community is possible only when love is the organizing principle.[5] It was this unity of love that Paul was commending to the Corinthians, for Paul believed that the love of God in Christ Jesus was the sole authentic foundation for all human relationships. The unconditional love described in chapter 13 is the perfect love of Christ, a goal to which we may aspire but can never reach.

The renowned Catholic theologian Karl Rahner built upon Paul's theology of love, but with a breathtaking twist. Rahner recognized that human beings are broken creatures. Left to our own devices, we are incapable of unconditional love. No matter how we might try, we can neither muster nor warrant such deep devotion. That is where God enters in.

Real love is a gift from God, a gift that has been given to all people through Jesus Christ. When we allow ourselves to receive this gift, we begin to understand what the old Sunday school song proclaimed—that Jesus loves *all* the little children of the world. Awash in the love of God, our only response is to love God in return. The trick is that God cannot be the direct object of our devotion. The Holy One is not some "target sized" being we can locate and adore. So our unconditional love of God must be transformed, or transferred, into a deep and fierce love of neighbor.

5   Richard B. Hays, *First Corinthians* (John Knox Press: Louisville, 1997), 222.

And what a love it is! As one scholar explained: "[Rahner] is thinking of neither romantic gestures and great acts, nor of moments of affection and mutual goodwill. He is thinking, rather, of those instances when we put another's interests before our own, when we stand by someone when it would be easier and pleasanter to leave, when we trust another person with our own selves and when we, in turn, are truly open to the unknown and uncontrollable reality of another person's identity."[6]

The beauty of Rahner's theology is this: We do not feel God's love when other people love us. Instead, Rahner believes we experience God's love when we love others. God's perfect love enters our hearts and flows into the world the moment we choose not to complain about how the shelves are dusted, or choose not to fuss about what songs are played for a wedding, or choose to stand by someone in a moment of weakness and need. This is the nature and source of unconditional love.

Strangely enough, the song "One" comes to much the same conclusion. The song moves from despairing over the flawed relationship to a recognition of what holds the couple, and all people, together. With echoes of Rahner and Paul, Bono sings:

> One love
> One blood
> One life
> You got to do what you should
> One life
> With each other
> Sisters
> Brothers
> One life
> But we're not the same
> We get to carry each other
> Carry each other
> One

First Congregational Church (UCC)
Moorhead, Minnesota
Valentine's Day

6 Shannon Craigo-Snell, "Redeeming Silence: Resources in Rahner for Contemporary Questions," Ph.D. diss., Yale University, 2002, 126–7.

fire

> *Abba Lot went to see Abba Joseph and said*
> *to him, "Abba, as far as I can, I say my little*
> *office, I fast a little, I pray and meditate, I live*
> *in peace and as far as I can, I purify my*
> *thoughts. What else can I do?" Then the old*
> *man stood up and stretched his hands towards*
> *heaven. His fingers became like ten lamps of*
> *fire and he said to him, "If you will, you*
> *can become all flame."*
>
> — Sayings of the Desert Fathers[1]

I knew my life was a mess, so I gave it up. It was out of control. I'd been burned, and the neighbors had gotten scared. I gathered stone, made a circle, drowned the flame. The ash would show them: It was safe, and I was sorry.

I expected that you expected me to be good, so I tried to do nothing bad. I expected that you expected me to be holy, so I stayed away from the wild man in the desert, the loose woman in the marketplace, the wanderer spitting in the mud beside the blind beggar. When the teachers said my gaze burned, I pulled the veil across my face and kept my eyes down.

I was in the courtyard of the Temple when I heard the call: "Be a living sacrifice." But I didn't feel alive, and the priests would not let me approach the altar.

So I ran into the wind; it rushed through heart and soul. The veil fell, ash cleared.

Now I run barefoot in the desert, the spark you set inside me calling to the pillar of flame ahead. We runners are a strange lot; carrying nothing but what cannot be left behind, we share what we find, following a fire so brilliant that we see it best reflected in each other's eyes.

Sarah Dylan Breuer

---

1 *The Sayings of the Desert Fathers: The Alphabetical Collection*, trans. Benedicta Ward, SLG (Kalamazoo, Michigan: Cistercian Publications Inc., 1984, 1975), 103.

Lent, Part One

Beth Maynard

Song reference: "God Part 2"
Biblical reference: Matthew 4:1–11

I first saw U2 in 1987 during the *Joshua Tree* tour—when they were the biggest band in the world for the first time. (Right now is the second time.) Back then, they had long hair and wore jeans, crosses, and flinty, righteous expressions. They sang about two great taboos, God and politics, and I thought they were cool.

When I heard they were playing the old Boston Garden, I got a ticket (I won't tell you how). While waiting for the show to begin, I struck up a conversation with the guy next to me. He asked if I had ever seen U2 live before.

When I told him I hadn't, he shook his head in envy. "I wish I could recapture that moment," he told me. "You will remember this night for the rest of your life." I asked why, and he said, "Have you ever been to church?" Seemed like a strange question, but it turned out to be a U2 cliché, started by their frontman Bono who would ask the audience the same thing, and then explain, "This is church!"

And boy, was it ever. I learned at that 1987 concert what many people learned during U2's 2001 Elevation tour: Whatever flaws there may be in that band, they can deliver on religious ecstasy. And people love them for it—their cosmic joy in life and love and God. Songs that soar with language like: It's a beautiful day, don't let it get away. Elevation, jubilation, revelation for the soul nation. Walk on, walk on, what you've got they can't deny it, can't sell it or buy it. *Gloria in te Domine; Gloria, exsultate.*

We Episcopalians pride ourselves on offering a participatory, sensory liturgical experience that we boast is not a mere performance but the "work" of the people. If we ever want to witness every one of those things taken to the max, we could do it at a U2 concert. During one climactic song, the house is lit up so you can see yourself and 29,999 of your closest friends jumping up and down with your hands in the air, like the heavens have opened, while Bono appears for all the world to be actually experiencing the beatific vision over at stage right. It's heady stuff.

And it was that heady stuff, that positive uplift that drew so much attention to the U2 I saw and wept with at the Boston Garden in 1987, and to the U2 I saw and wept with at the Providence Civic Center in 2001. But of course, what draws attention is never the whole story, and the problem with getting known as "the uplifting band" is that some people, especially their many Christian fans, expect U2 to be nice, pure, and free of dark sides. Well, in case you are laboring under that misapprehension, about them or anybody else—including yourself!—our epistle today will remind you that *all* have sinned.

One of my favorite U2 songs is a lesser-known one which deals precisely with what it's like to face our own sin. For a band whose early work was pretty heavy on uncritically happy pro-Jesus anthems, it is rather brilliantly titled "God Part 2." Written in tribute to John Lennon and full of Lennon references, the song is built around a searing confession of hypocrisy. It takes every bit of moral merit anyone has ever ascribed to Bono the singer or U2 the band, rips it apart, and leaves it lying in shreds on the floor. "I don't believe the devil, I don't believe his book," it begins, "but the truth is not the same without the lies he made up."

"God Part 2" always reminds me of the Ash Wednesday confession,[2] which we prayed together just four days ago,

2 *The Book of Common Prayer* (New York: Church Hymnal Corporation, 1977), 268.

where we stop hedging about vague "things" we've "done and left undone" and actually cut to the bone with prayers like "our blindness to human need and suffering, our indifference to injustice and cruelty, we confess to you, Lord." Bono sings, "I don't believe in excess; success is to give. I don't believe in riches, but you should see where I live." "Our anger at our own frustration," we pray, "and the pride, hypocrisy and impatience of our lives, we confess to you, Lord." "I don't believe in cocaine," howls Bono, "but I've got a speedball in my head. I could cut and crack you open. Did you hear what I said?"

As the music gets wilder, the voice jumps an octave to name things it's lost faith in, ruling out options where a less introspective person might find solace and hope: good ol' rock and roll, for example, or that whole spirit of the 1960s our elders tried to tell us was so magic. Hypocrisy is carrying the day and the song is spinning out of control—weird whooshing noises of collapse joining with the increasingly frantic drum track and the singer's drowning cries for rescue.

It doesn't end there, but I'm going to push the pause button for a minute.

No one could ever, would ever, write this kind of song without having known God first, but the kind of insight into hypocrisy it displays only comes when you've moved into knowing God, Part 2.

Now, there's a Part 2 aspect to our Gospel today as well. So let's do a flashback to Part 1. Do you remember what happened right before this story? It was the day Jesus was baptized. The heavens were opened, and he had the beatific vision, and 29,999 of his closest friends were jumping up and down at the River Jordan as the Spirit descended and a voice said, "You're my beloved!"

Today's gospel reading is Part 2, after that uncritically happy early stuff. Part 2, where you eventually must go sometime after your life gets opened to God, at least if you want it to stay open. We read this Part 2 story on the first Sunday in Lent every single year: Jesus hearing the voice of the devil so soon after he's heard the voice of God.

Right after his peak baptism experience, Matthew tells us, "Jesus was led up by the Spirit into the wilderness to be tempted." Starving, sleep-deprived, sweat pouring down his sides, doubting the things other people say should give him hope, Jesus looks in the eyes of evil. He recognizes what he could do if he chose wrongly, how he could abuse his power. He says no, three times, but the fight is a real one. That's meant to inspire us, not scandalize us. Don't we want a Jesus who has to fight? Who understands when we have to tell him, yet again, "I don't believe the devil, *but* . . ."

I want a Jesus who has been in the mud, in whose presence Lent becomes more than a time for congratulating ourselves on giving up chocolate, who will fight for us as we drag our own experiences of evil out into the light. I want a Jesus whose church is a place you can get changed, not a club for nice people (or people trying to pretend they're nice). I need to hear the voice of God, but I also need to admit that sometimes I hear the voice of evil. It is, really, a dangerous mistake to try and face only the light without also facing the darkness that is inside you. It is a dangerous mistake to try and stockpile clean water while pretending there is no mud around your feet.

You know that as well as I do. We all know perfectly well that the mud is as real as the water, the darkness as real as the light. But so often we're too embarrassed and too phony to bring it to church. Well, I want to tell you that church is where it belongs. Hiding it from God is what gives it power. Exposing it to God is what heals and integrates it.

If you want proof, let me take the pause button off that song now. Do you remember where we left off? The world was coming apart to a drum track. The singer was screaming out for hope in the face of the hypocrisy he'd exposed.

At the very last moment, just before the song screeches to a halt, he finds it. Or better, it finds him, and he marvels: "When I feel like I'm falling, like I'm spinning on a wheel, it always stops beside a name, a presence I can feel . . . I believe in love." The ending is incredibly abrupt: one Name, one tangible Presence—Jesus shows up, and hope comes with him. The chaos is over. Evil is still real, but it has no ultimate power next to the power of Love.

That's what happens when an honest hypocrite comes to church. And this is church.

If you look at your own hypocrisy as hard as U2 does in this song, you'll probably end up feeling like you're spinning, too, irredeemably fake, stuck in Ash Wednesday, screaming out for hope.

So where is it? Do you know where it is? Is it in anything you can do? Is it in trying to be nicer? Trying to pretend you already are nicer? No, baby, it's in Love. It's in the Love that hung on the cross caked with mud and sweat for you. Just bring your own mud and sweat on up here and believe in Love.

"When I feel like I'm falling, like I'm spinning on a wheel, it always stops beside one name, a presence I can feel."

Fake niceness is not more powerful than real evil. But the real Jesus is more powerful than anything.

Radio Sermon, Cathedral Church of St. Paul
Boston, Massachusetts
Lent 1, Year A

Grace the Beauty-Maker

Wade Hodges

Song reference: "Grace"
Biblical reference: Romans 5

*It's a powerful idea, grace. It really is. And, you
know, we hear so much of karma and so little of
grace. Every religion teaches us about karma
and, well, what you put out you will receive.
And even Christianity, which is supposed to be
about grace, has turned, you know, redemption
into good manners, or the right accent, or, you
know, good works or whatever it is. I just can't
get over grace—(it's) so hard to find.*

— Bono (to Launch.com, 10/18/2001)

I t's been said that "In the gospel, we discover that we are
worse off than we thought, and far more loved than we ever
dreamed."[3] This is just one more way of saying that in the
gospel we discover the grace of God.

---

3 Steven Curtis Chapman and Scotty Smith, *Speechless: Living in Awe
of God's Disruptive Grace* (Grand Rapids, MI: Zondervan, 1999).

Grace is the theological word used to describe this incredible love that God pours out on undeserving creatures like us. In his book, *What's So Amazing About Grace,* Philip Yancey describes grace as the "last best word" in the English language. It's one of the few theological words that have yet to be spoiled or sullied by the hypocrisy of those who preach them or the cynicism of those who reject them. Grace is still a beautiful word. Still a compelling thought. Still marvelous to experience.

Bono's fascination with grace led him to describe it in a song, as only a poet can:

> Grace, she takes the blame
> She covers the shame
> Removes the stain
> It could be her name
>
> Grace, it's the name for a girl
> It's also a thought that changed the world
>
> What once was hurt
> What once was friction
> What left a mark
> No longer stings
> Because Grace makes beauty
> Out of ugly things
> Grace makes beauty out of ugly things.

Grace is not the norm in our world. In our world, where *quid pro quo* reigns, where you get what you deserve, where what goes around comes around, where enemies stand toe to toe making sure every strike is given an appropriate counterstrike, you have to look hard for grace. When you do find it, it will blow you away. It will send you reeling. You'll struggle to make sense of it. Your best efforts at articulating it to others will always fall short.

A man who walked unscathed from a gruesome automobile accident was asked by his pastor to give a testimony the next Sunday. As the man recounted what happened that day and how easily he could have been killed, he was overcome with emotion. With great joy in his voice, he shouted these final words to the congregation before taking his seat, "If it weren't for the grace of God, I'd be in heaven right now!" Yes, grace has caused many of us to lose our heads. Why shouldn't it? It's not like anything else in this world. In Bono's words, it "travels outside of karma." It isn't deserved. It's simply received. In its simplicity, grace has the ability to change the world.

Grace makes beauty out of ugly things.

You don't have to watch CNN all day long to realize how challenging it is to get two enemies to lay their weapons aside and reconcile. You don't have to be Colin Powell to understand how difficult the peace process is. You don't have to watch Ben Affleck and Samuel Jackson go at each other in *Changing Lanes* to get a sense of how much more seductive retaliation is than mercy.

Yet, in Romans 5:1, Paul says that through Jesus Christ, we now have peace with our God. Mercy has been given. We have been reconciled with the one against whom we've rebelled. What makes peace with God a possibility? A reality? You guessed it—grace.

> You see, at just the right time, when we were still powerless, Christ died for the ungodly. Very rarely will anyone die for a righteous man, though for a good man someone might possibly dare to die. But God demonstrates his own love for us in this: While we were still sinners, Christ died for us.
>
> Since we have now been justified by his blood, how much more shall we be saved from God's wrath through him! For if, when we were God's enemies, we were reconciled to him through the death of his Son, how much more, having been reconciled, shall we be saved through his life! Not only is this so, but we also rejoice in God through our Lord Jesus Christ, through whom we have now received reconciliation. (Rom. 5:6–11, NIV)

The gospel can be summarized in two statements: People fail, and God loves us anyway. God's love for us runs so strong, God's desire for us reaches so deep, that while we stood aligned against him with a weapon in our hand, he sent his Son to die for us, as a way of extending mercy and making peace. Imagine Arafat or Sharon doing such a thing for the other, and you'll begin to understand why after all these years of reflection and study, the word "amazing" is still the best anybody can do when describing God's grace.

Grace makes beauty out of ugly things. Our sin is huge. Its consequences are massive. Our rebellion has made a terrible mess of this world. But as large as our sin is, it cannot overshadow the grace of God. There is nothing we can do to make God stop loving us. There is no sin so great as to disqualify us from the opportunity to be reconciled. As our sin increases, God's grace increases all the more. God will not let sin have the last word in His story. No matter how far and wide the stain spreads, or how ugly it gets, God's grace is always big enough to cover the blemish and creative enough to make beauty out of something ugly.

One of my favorite movies, for reasons my wife cannot understand, is *Fight Club.* In one of the more important scenes of the movie, Tyler Durden, played by Brad Pitt, says to Edward Norton's character:

> Our fathers were our models for God. Our fathers bailed. What does that tell you about God? You have to consider the possibility that God doesn't like you. He doesn't want you. In all probability, he hates you. . . .We don't need him. [Forget about] damnation. [Forget about] redemption. If we are God's unwanted children, so be it.

From the cross, God shouts an anticipatory response to Tyler Durden and all those who have ever caught themselves thinking what he said. From the cross, the gospel message blares. God doesn't hate us. God doesn't want to count us as his enemies. God doesn't want to annihilate us. God doesn't want to punish us. God wants to save us. God wants to bless us. God wants to forgive us. God wants to call us his friends. God wants to live in harmony with his children for eternity.

God will do whatever it takes to hammer this truth home. If leading us out of the fog of rebellion requires the sacrifice of his Son, then he'll do it. If softening our hardened hearts requires the death of an innocent on behalf of the guilty, then so be it.

That's how much we mean to him.
That's how much he loves us.
That's what grace caused him to do.
That's how God makes beauty out of ugly things.

The Sterling Drive Church
Bellingham, Washington
21 April 2002

Dying to Live

Leslie J. Reinke

Song reference: "Gone" (concert lyrics)
Biblical references: Matthew 13:44–46; 1 John 2:17

The Kingdom of the Heavens is like treasure buried in the open country, which a man finds, but buries again, and, in his joy about it, goes and sells all he has and buys that piece of ground. Again the Kingdom of the Heavens is like a jewel merchant who is in quest of choice pearls. He finds one most costly pearl; he goes away; and though it costs all he has, he buys it."[4]

Jim Elliott (1927–1956) was an American college student who developed a radical lifestyle of faith based on his relationship with Jesus. In the prime of his life, he came to believe that God wanted him to share the message of the

---

4   Matthew 13:44–46, in Richard F. Weymouth, *New Testament in Modern Speech,* third edition, rev. and ed. E. Hampden-Cooke (1912).

"Kingdom of the Heavens" with the Auca Indians of Ecuador. The Aucas (currently known as the Huaorani) were feared and left alone because of their ruthless behavior toward outsiders. Nevertheless, Jim and four like-minded companions arrived in Ecuador, learned the local languages, and traveled to the remote location where the Aucas lived. However, while attempting to befriend the Aucas, the five young men were ambushed and massacred.

As news of the killings spread, many people were shocked by what seemed like a senseless waste of life. But several years earlier Jim had written these words in his journal: "He is no fool who gives what he cannot keep to gain what he cannot lose."[5] These were not idle words; Jim died as he had lived, believing that even his physical life was not too great a price to pay in order to gain the treasures of "the Kingdom of the Heavens." He believed that "the world, with its cravings, is passing away, but he who does God's will continues for ever."[6]

Jesus once told some stories that illustrate the truth that it can be an astute transaction to exchange all that one has in order to acquire something of far greater worth. Jesus was referring to the incomparable value of being a part of "the Kingdom of the Heavens," the term he used to describe the condition of being in perfect harmony with the all-encompassing God.[7] When Jesus spoke of "the Kingdom of the Heavens," he referred not only the place we call "Heaven," but also to an environment without limits. The rule of God is intended to extend everywhere; nothing is to be excluded. And rather than regarding this as an onerous burden, one can instead discover it to be the way to freedom and release. It is the very joy of this discovery that would prompt a person to abandon possessions, ambitions, and pursuits in order to embrace—and be embraced by—the King of this Kingdom.

---

5   The story of the life and death of Jim Elliot and his companions is told by Elisabeth Elliot in the book *Through Gates of Splendor.*
6   1 John 2:17, *New Testament in Modern Speech.*
7   Sometimes the original words are translated into English as "the kingdom of heaven," leaving one to think that what is being referred to is a far-away, mystical place. However, a more correct rendering is "the kingdom of the heavens." "The heavens" was a Hebrew concept that extended from the far reaches of outer space to the very air that one breathed; as such, it included everything around and beyond us.

In these parables, a person finds a treasure and liquidates all his assets in order to acquire it. The point is not that the person is impoverished by such a transaction; rather, the worth of the acquired treasure far exceeds its purchase price. Thus, the person is seen as wise and shrewd.

It seems so idealistic. We find a similar truth expressed in U2's song "Gone" from their 1997 album *Pop*. Although this song did not gain much commercial airplay, to me it is one of U2's best. U2's lyrics are sometimes maddeningly ambiguous, suggesting different things to different people, but to me these words speak to the deep truth of Jesus' teachings about the "Kingdom of the Heavens":

> You get to feel so guilty
> Got so much for so little
> Then you find that feeling just won't go away.
> You are holding on to every little thing so tightly
> You wanted to get somewhere so badly
> You had to lose yourself along the way.

The song speaks of a person who has experienced a significant measure of success in life. But the person finds that in the process of becoming successful, he has become a greedy, grasping, selfish person: "What you thought was freedom is just greed." He is enveloped by guilt. He feels that he has lost himself, that he has had to compromise his beliefs and values and character in order to get ahead. He recognizes that his possessions have come to possess him. He has alienated those whom he loves. Although at the beginning he did not consider this cost too great, looking back, he regrets the price he has paid to achieve his goals.

Then this person evidently has an experience that transforms his life. He reaches a point where he is almost relieved to leave behind all of his accomplishments in order to embrace something of far greater value.

> Goodbye, you can keep this suit of lights
> I'll be up with the sun
> I'm not coming down, I'm not coming down, I'm not coming down.

He sees his former emptiness and has no regrets about leaving it all behind. He'd rather be "up with the sun," closer to you every day." Thus "Gone" echoes the story of Jim Elliot, someone whose encounter with the living Jesus so transformed his life that now he is "up with the Sun"—Jesus, the Sun of Righteousness, who brings light into our sin-darkened world, who made a way to reconcile God with a lost humanity. The person in the song invites the listener to join him but defiantly adds that even if he has to travel alone, he's "not coming down." He has made his decision, and there is no turning back.

This is an incredibly joyful and exuberant song, one whose melody complements the soaring, passionate vocals. But mostly, it is a song of hope, the same hope that we find in Jesus' stories—hope that lost people can be found, that enslaved people can be set free, that the seemingly wasted can be redeemed, and that true treasures are not out of reach.

13 January 2003

A Turning Point

Amy Lincoln

Song reference: "Walk On"
Biblical references: Genesis 8:13–22; 9:8–17;
Isaiah 43:1–3

A couple of weeks ago my husband Jeff and I went to see the band U2 in concert at Madison Square Garden. Their music has shaped my generation, and I was excited to see them live for the first time. I did not anticipate how powerful an experience it would be to hear this particular band in New York City so soon after September 11. In light of the terrorist attacks, many of their lyrics struck me as prophetic.

On the day of the concert, Jeff had walked to Ground Zero. Smoke was still rising in the air, choking him. But later, U2 sang words of hope: "I see the dust cloud disappear without a trace." They sang words of encouragement:

> If the daylight feels like it's a long way off,
> and if your glass heart should crack
> and for a second you turn back
> Oh no, be strong.
>
> Walk on, walk on
> Stay safe tonight.

They sang of an impatient longing for peace:

Heaven on earth
we need it now
I'm sick of all of this hanging around
Sick of sorrow
Sick of pain
Sick of hearing again and again
That there's gonna be
Peace on earth.

This concert was a healing. The lyrics and music resonated in my soul, and my tears fell for the way the world has changed.

U2, who learned firsthand about terrorism and war by watching the turmoil in Northern Ireland, makes music that ministers. They respond faithfully to a call from God. In that particular place and time, in the midst of a palpably broken world, they brought a powerful healing message to us all.

Our text today takes us back to the world's brokenness in another time, that of Noah in the Old Testament. God is fed up with the faithlessness of just about every living thing on Earth. The situation seems hopeless, so God decides to destroy the world with a flood. The story of Noah's Ark is familiar to us through adorable animals adorning baby nurseries and children's songs, but when you really think about it, this is *not* a kids' story! If you really read and digest it, it is an unsettling biblical account of the almost total devastation of God's creation—by God! The very same God who, only a few chapters earlier, had declared creation to be "good."

In chapter six of Genesis it is written, "The Lord saw that the wickedness of humankind was great in the earth, and that every inclination of the thoughts of their hearts was only evil continually. And the Lord was sorry that he had made humankind on the earth, and it grieved him to his heart. So the Lord said, 'I will blot out from the earth the human beings I have created—people together with animals and creeping things and birds of the air, for I am sorry that I have made them.'"

This account of God's response of judgment toward creation is troubling, but in his commentary on Genesis, Walter Brueggemann suggests that "the resolution is not by God's indulgence of his anger. Nor is it by indulgence of the hostile creation or by some change in creation. Rather, the resolution comes by the resolve of God's heart to fashion a newness."[8] This was a turning point in history—a new beginning. The grace here is that God does not fully turn away from creation; God saves a remnant from the waters of the flood. Noah is singled out by God as the only righteous one in this generation and is saved.

In creation, God freely chose to fashion a relationship with the earth and all that is in it and with human beings, created in God's image. God doesn't need humans, but God chooses us. And here in the story of Noah, God again chooses to remain in relationship with the earth and all that is in it and human beings, despite their sinfulness. This is an important turning point, for it is here that God makes a covenant never to destroy the earth and all flesh again. "The granting of a unilateral peace treaty by God is rooted in the divine heartache over creation."[9]

This assurance is perhaps more important to us now, after September 11, than it has ever seemed before. It is not that evil has been eradicated from creation, but that "we are now assured that [death and destruction] are not rooted in the anger or rejection of God."[10] This is the importance of the covenant—the "never again" resolution of God. The terrorist attacks are not something that God caused because of our collective sin, to teach us a lesson or to bring us closer together, as some have said. No! God is for us and loves us, and through God's power, good can come out of evil. Noah's story marks the turning point, and the covenant marks God's intention never again to destroy creation.

The flood that Noah survives is fundamentally different than the destruction and loss of life of September 11. It is different because in the biblical narrative of Noah, it is God who initiates the flood. But the September 11 attacks are an expression not of God's wrath but of *human* sinfulness. God's covenant still stands.

---

8   Walter Brueggemann, *Genesis* (Atlanta: John Knox Press, 1982), 80.
9   Thomas W. Mann, *The Book of the Torah: The Narrative Integrity of the Pentateuch* (Atlanta: John Knox Press, 1971), 22.
10 Bruggemann, 84.

I heard a sermon preached recently in which the pastor dismissed the horror of that awful day by essentially saying, "Well, it could've been worse." Many more people could have died if the planes and buildings were full. That minister said he believed that God was with those people who survived—those who were running late, those who missed their planes. But what about the faith of those who died? Wasn't God with them too?

That minister failed in his theology; he failed in his pastoral duty. But in their concert in New York City, U2 did what that minister failed to do: They created a space for New York City and for all of America to cry out in anguish for our deep loss. The songs they sang that night pierced through our emotional armor and worked in our hearts and through our tears. They drew us together as a community of mourners, living in pain yet seeking hope.

At that concert, U2's lyrics and passion reminded me of the hope that God offers to us out of the ruins, in the midst of the wilderness. God has made a covenant, a binding agreement, something we can count on, never again to cause the devastation of the earth. And we are covenant people, heirs of the promise God made, symbolized by the rainbow. And God has promised:

Do not fear, for I have redeemed you;
I have called you by name, you are mine.
When you pass through the waters, I will be with you;
and through the rivers, they shall not overwhelm you;
when you walk through fire you shall not be burned,
and the flame shall not consume you.
For I am the Lord your God,
the Holy One of Israel, your Savior. (Isa. 43:1–3)

In the face of human sin, in the face of overwhelming evil, these promises enable us to walk on, through the pain, through the loss, through the fear, to walk on into new life and the everlasting arms of God.

Hilltop Church
Mendham, New Jersey
Fall 2001

An Army of One

Mike Kinman

Song reference: "Pride (in the name of love)"
Biblical reference: Mark 14

One man come in the name of love
One man come and go.
One man come he to justify
One man to overthrow

In the name of love. What more in the name
of love?

Palm Sunday is the beginning of a journey. For many of us, it's a familiar one, but just as we can see things differently by walking the same route that in the past we've always driven, I'm hoping that a change of perspective can turn a familiar journey into a new adventure, one that might even change our lives.

You probably noticed something different about the way we read the Passion Gospel this year. Usually, after all the individual roles are assigned, the rest of the congregation gets to play the crowd. Most of the gathered community's role, therefore, is to stand in judgment over Christ and shout the indicting line "Crucify him!"

There is a logic to this. First, there's the simple practical logic of having the crowd actually performed by a crowd. But beyond that, there's the powerful experience of seeing ourselves as the empire, as the oppressor, and of hearing our own voice call for Christ's crucifixion and denying his Lordship over our lives. I've always experienced it as profoundly painful, recognizing and owning the ways in which I deny Christ in my life through my self-centered actions and through my participation in a society that is, despite many good intentions, more oppressor than oppressed, and more like the Roman Empire than any other nation-state since Rome itself fell.

This year, however, the congregation read the part of Christ. I didn't shift the roles because I think the message we get from being the crowd is wrong or too uncomfortable. I switched the roles because, although I believe it is important to occasionally stand in the role of the crowd as a corrective, it is not our proper role this week or for the rest of the year.

Holy Week, and in fact our whole life as disciples of Christ, is not about us beating ourselves up over being Christ-killers. It's about us being the once-and-still broken, the now-and-forever resurrected Body of Christ on earth. Holy Week is about us as that Body of Christ re-membering—literally putting back together, taking the past and making it present again—re-membering Christ's walk from his entry into Jerusalem, his last supper with his friends, his lonely vigil in the garden, his trial, his abandonment, his crucifixion, his death, and finally his resurrection—re-membering it not as witness to it, but as it happens to us.

As Christians, we do not mourn that we have killed Christ—we take up the cross and rejoice in our identity as the Body of Christ.

This particular Palm Sunday, we cannot escape the irony of re-enacting Christ's triumphal entry into the holy and ancient city of Jerusalem riding on a donkey at the same time our own nation is making its triumphant entry into another holy and ancient city in tanks and armored personnel carriers. It is made even more ironic by the recruiting slogan of our armed forces, "an Army of one."

A moment ago I recited to you the lyrics of the song "Pride (In the Name of Love)" by U2. "One man come in the name of love. One man come and go. One man come he to justify. One man to overthrow. In the name of love. What more in the name of love?"

Jesus rode into and out of Jerusalem acclaimed by a crowd that in a matter of days would deride him and sentence him to death. The reason for their change of heart is the difference between the army that is parading through Baghdad's streets this night and the army of one that entered the gates of Jerusalem. Both came to justify. Both came to overthrow. But their driving force was different. Only Jesus' pride was in the name, not of nation or self-aggrandizement, but of love. And the crowd didn't think that one man come in the name of love was an army that was going to do what they wanted—so they turned on him and took his life.

The greatest irony, though, and our greatest hope, is that Christ has actually shown that one person coming in the name of love truly is an army. Jesus, betrayed by his own friend with a kiss, abandoned by most of the rest of his friends and beaten and killed on the cross, had a greater effect on history than anyone before or since. Those who followed in his footsteps, who had the courage to be armies of one coming in the name of love, did likewise. Mahatma Gandhi was one, and he overthrew an empire with active, loving, nonviolent resistance. They took his life, too.

Martin Luther King, Jr., too, was "one man come in the name of love." He engaged the conscience of a nation and opened its eyes to the evils of racism. He helped set in motion a tide of justice that still rolls today. And as U2 remembers, a "shot rings out in the Memphis sky" on April 4, 1968. It indeed did take his life, but it did not take a pride, an identity, a vision that was not about himself but about love. In the name of love.

As Christians, we believe that Christ gave himself up for the sake of the world, and it is that act that is our salvation—not because a price was paid for us but because a way was shown and an identity was given to us. We are the Body of Christ. We have no higher calling. We have no truer identity. We have no more daunting challenge. We have no more profound joy.

This week that leads up to Easter is about living intentionally, every day, every hour, every moment, for seven days, in contemplation of who we are and what it means to be one body, the Body of Christ, that comes in the name of love.

On Palm Sunday it means riding with Christ among people who are ready to make us queens and kings—for the price of our souls—and having the courage to turn down our own glory for the sake of God and in the name of love.

On Maundy Thursday it means kneeling with Christ, washing each other's feet and committing ourselves to serve rather than be served. It means breaking the bread and passing the cup with Christ, and experiencing Eucharist not as a matter of our individual comfort and nourishment but as an action we do in the way it was done for us and for all humankind—not for our sake but for the sake of the world.

On Good Friday it means receiving the blows and hanging on the cross with Christ, struggling with the difficult call to stand up for love, refusing to back down, and even forgiving those who persecute us for it.

On Holy Saturday it means lying in the tomb with Christ, wondering if everything we have done, all the sacrifices we have made have really been a huge mistake—the biggest mistake we could ever make.

And on Easter Sunday it means rising to new life with Christ, bringing light and life and hope to the world, feeling the joy of the victory of love, and in the words of that old protest song that Dr. King and so many others have sung before us, knowing that "deep in our hearts, we do believe." We believe not only that "we shall overcome someday," but that by Christ and with Christ and in Christ we already have.

We are members of the Body of Christ. We are each an army of one, and together an army of One Body, and we come in the name of love.

This week, let us claim our pride in the name of love, let us walk with Christ and see what love has already done. Let us sit in awe and wonder and contemplate what love is doing right now. And as Easter dawns and we breathe in the air of resurrected life, let us look back at where we've been. Let us look forward, too, at the world that is set before us. And let us ask what more Christ calls this army of one, and each of our armies of one, to do and be.

What more in the name of love?

Episcopal Campus Ministry
Washington University
St. Louis, Missouri
Palm Sunday, Year B
13 April 2003

"Woo me, sister; move me, brother!" What does Pop Culture Have to Do with Preaching?

Raewynne J. Whiteley

It's about time! Let me know when it's out!" It's been a common reaction, from U2 fans and preachers alike, to the announcement of this book. A very different reaction has also been common: a perplexed frown, an uncomfortable laugh, a look of blank incomprehension. "Preaching U2? What do you mean?"

While some people have no doubt about the wisdom of placing U2 and faith side by side, for others it is a struggle. What has U2 got to do with religion? What has popular culture got to do with the gospel?

In a culture where religion belongs to the private world and pop culture to the public, we have tended to think of religion and pop culture as two areas divided by a vast chasm. On the one side, fans fear contamination of their life-giving pop culture with life-denying pulpit prognostications; on the other, preachers hark back with puritanical disapproval to the excesses of "sex, drugs, and rock 'n' roll," the music of the devil.

But in spite of our mutual suspicions, the reality is that religion and pop culture have always been connected. In the medieval period, mystery plays and their accompanying, and often bawdy, music taught the great themes of Christian theology to the uneducated; in the sixteenth century, hymn tunes were derived from tavern songs. Even in the twentieth century, faith has frequently found expression, or at least come under examination, in popular music, whether in the influence of gospel music on jazz and blues or the explicit questioning of a song like Joan Osborne's "One of Us." And we have also seen the rise of a whole new genre of "Christian music," along with the proliferation of multi-media worship experiences.

And so the relationships between religion and pop culture have tended to take one of two paths—mutual abhorrence (as described above) or unconditional appropriation (borrowing the trappings of religion for a multi-media "spiritual" effect, or trying to add the beats of pop music to Christian hymns "to attract the young people"). However, neither of these responses does full justice to the integral and substantial relationship between religion and culture.

The twentieth century saw a huge shift in the place of Christianity in the world. In 1900, the balance of power was held by the Christian capitalist west, the so-called "first world." Colonialism and Christianity went hand in hand, and there was a more or less unified Christian world view. A hundred years later, the scene had changed dramatically. The dramatic growth of the Christian community in Latin and South America, Africa, Asia and Oceania, and a parallel shrinking of Christian influence in the former colonial powers, changed the balance of power. While the content of the gospel remained constant (albeit with greater attention to issues of justice), its expression varied across different cultures. We began to recognize pluralism in world views, even among Christians, and it became impossible to ignore the reality of religion and culture influencing one another.[1]

Religion looks different in different places and cultures. Geography can shape theology. If you grow up in northern Europe, where Christmas falls in the dead of winter, Christ

---

1   Robert Schreiter, *Constructing Local Theologies* (Maryknoll, NY: Orbis Books, 1985), xi.

the light of the world has different associations attached to it than it does in Australia, where Christmas is accompanied by the fierce summer sun.

Likewise, the prophecy of Amos, "I hate, I despise your festivals, and I take no delight in your solemn assemblies . . . Take away from me the noise of your songs; I will not listen to the melody of your harps. But let justice roll down like waters, and righteousness like an ever-flowing stream"(5:21, 23-24) carries a myriad of different associations if it is read in Westminster Abbey, than if read in the refugee camps of Jenin or the Gaza strip.

The story from Acts 2 of the new Christians selling what they have and holding all in common is regarded as challenging at the least, or plain unrealistic, in New York City; in a culture where the primary unit is the village, rather than the individual, or in a monastery, it has a ring of authenticity.

And Paul's admonition to women to cover their heads when prophesying might well be liberating to a woman who has grown up wearing the veil in Afghanistan because it gives her permission to prophesy; but outrageous to a graduate of Vassar[2] who cannot imagine any restriction on her speech.

The examples are endless. But what is common to all is the way in which religion and culture influence one another. However, that relationship is rarely made explicit. We tend to assume that the way we understand and do things is universal, that everyone is like that. We are all too often unaware of the ways in which our own geographical and cultural contexts, and, indeed, our own histories, shape the way we do faith.

But the influence is not just in one direction. Culture critiques and shapes faith; faith critiques and shapes culture. The relationship is dialectical—as we pay attention to a specific instance of the influence of culture on faith, we become aware of where that influence has itself been shaped by faith, and so on, in a never-ending dance.

And this happens not so much on a formal level, in the councils of the church, but on an informal level, in the lives and communities of the faithful, from which it trickles up to the structures. People grab hold of their culture in one hand and their religion in the other, and then try to work out how it is that they can not only co-exist, but be in harmony. They

---

2   A small, elite college in Poughkeepsie, New York.

ask questions and forge answers, they look for places of genuine coherence, for authentic emotion, for congruity with experience. Both culture and religion tap into the very essence of who we are; they are the building blocks of our identity. It is no wonder, then, that they are integrally and substantially related.

And that is particularly true of the relationship between pop culture, as expressed in music, and Christian faith. Theologian Robert Schreiter suggests that "the poet, the prophet, the teacher . . . may be among those who give leadership to the actual shaping into words of the response of faith."[3] It is here that U2 belongs, along with the many preachers who have heard U2's work and struggled to give voice to the theologies which emerge from its interaction with the sacred. They give voice not only to their own longings and hopes, but to those of our culture alongside those of our tradition—so that we learn to speak a truly colloquial language of faith.

• • •

I still remember one of my first preaching classes in seminary. We sat in the classroom and used our fingers to count off a simple five-step model for preaching. State the point, explain the point, illustrate the point, apply the point, and finally, restate the point. Thumb, index finger, middle finger, ring finger, pinkie. Do this three times over, add an introduction and conclusion, and "Voilà!" You have a sermon.

But, of course, the whole process was based on a fallacy. A number of fallacies, actually. First of all, that preaching is a fundamentally propositional activity. Preaching is an expression of the word of God; it is one means by which God speaks to us here in the twenty-first century. And if the words of God in scripture are anything to go by, God is not limited to talking in propositions. God tells stories, God laments, God comforts, God celebrates. A robust understanding of preaching as the word of God means that we will not be content to talk in our sermons about God as if God were some abstract entity, but that we will strive to create a space in which God's very self can be heard, felt, experienced.

---

3   Schreiter, 17.

The second fallacy, evident from the separation of proposition/explanation and illustration/application, is that interpretation of the biblical text can be done in isolation from real life. The notion that one can, through study, prayer, or whatever, somehow objectively discern some idealized notion of truth is akin to doing surgery in a sterile environment without a patient—it defeats its very purpose. The problems raised are both theological and philosophical. Theologically speaking, as Christians we worship an incarnate God. God is neither an abstract principle nor a disembodied spirit. The uniqueness of our spiritual tradition is that we follow a God who became flesh and lived among us. This is a God who ate, slept, cried—and died—and in resurrection brought new life to us all. Christ did not simply preach the gospel; he *was* the gospel, the good news of God, who brought in his body wisdom and healing and forgiveness. His incarnation becomes the model for our life of faith—not some disembodied spirituality, but a gritty engagement with an embodied world in and through which God speaks. Our preaching must exhibit that same engagement if it to is to become a vehicle of the gospel, a vehicle of the grace of God. Christ is God "with skin"—and any attempt to preach "without skin," without an incarnational praxis, is to deny in ourselves the very thing God did in Christ.[4]

Philosophically speaking, what postmodernism has brought to light is that while objective truth may exist, we as human beings can only know it subjectively. This is a radical departure from previous notions of truth and of authority.[5] In premodern societies, the world was conceived of as a relational body, the basic unit being the community. The preacher embodied the community, and preached an authoritative and reliable corporate truth. In modernism, truth was determined not by its speaker, but by its correspondence with empirical observation. It was subject to the rules of logic,

---

4   For further reading see Alla Renee Bozarth, *The Word's Body: An Incarnational Aesthetic of Interpretation* (Lanham, MD: University Press of America, 1997), particularly chapters 3-4.

5   For further reading see Roland J. Allen, Barbara Shires Blaisdell, and Scott Black Johnston, *Theology for Preaching: Authority, Truth and Knowledge of God in a Postmodern Ethos* (Nashville: Abingdon Press, 1997), particularly the introduction and chapters 1-3.

objective, abstract, and universally valid. The preacher functioned as an objective observer who could in turn identify objective truth.

But postmodernism has undermined both premodernism and modernism. It identifies truth that might potentially exist, but which cannot be accessed directly and without mediation. All perception involves interpretation, and hence any truth is an interpreted truth, reflecting the lenses of our experience. So it is a mistake to assume that we as preachers can somehow access some objective theological truth, unshaped by our experience, and then convey it to others who will receive it objectively. We are all shaped by our culture and experiences; they make us truly human. Truth always comes to us in a particular (rather than universal) form, and is always in conversation with the world around us. Postmodernism is distrustful of claims of objectivity and of abstraction from life.

And so, from a postmodern perspective, it is impossible to interpret Scripture in isolation from real life. Our culture and experience will always be present and influential.

The reality is that this is nothing new. In preaching, we have always had multiple influences. In the past, we have tended to label them as "illustrations" or "the use of experience in preaching," but anyone who has ever tried to write a sermon with an "illustration" already ringing in their ears knows how that illustration shapes our reading from the very beginning of our work. The Christmas gospels always come to us laden with Christmas carols; I cannot read the Easter gospels without thinking of a friend who died one Easter morning, her last words "Christ is risen indeed." Similarly, we cannot look at our legal code without hearing echoes of the Ten Commandments; we cannot hear Shakespeare without noticing allusions to Scripture.

From a theoretical perspective, this mutual influence is called "intertextuality." Broadly simplified, this is the idea that every human utterance (or "text") is drawn from numerous other texts. Nothing we say is entirely new, nor is it entirely objective: It is all the result of the collision and influence

---

6 Julia Kristeva, *Desire in Language: A Semiotic Approach to Literature and Art*, ed. L. S. Roudiez, trans T. Gora, A. Jardine and L. S. Roudiez (New York, Columbia University Press, 1980), 66; Roland Barthes, *Image, Music, Text* (New York: Hill and Wang), 146.

of everything we have ever heard, read, and experienced. Every text is a mosaic or tissue of quotations.[6] Some of these influences are subtle, barely noticeable; others are strong, demanding our attention.

In terms of preaching, what this means is that alongside the biblical text are a whole bunch of other texts vying for our attention. They come from our family histories, our reading, the media, the world around us. They spill over into the biblical text, shape how we read it, and the text in turn shapes how they are understood to be meaningful. And then the whole muddle somehow (though hard work and the intervention of the Holy Spirit) coalesces into a new text, the one we call a sermon.

So when it comes to preaching, to follow a simple interpretation-illustration-application model is to ignore the riches of this intertextual web, and to make instead relatively superficial connections between text and some hypothetical lived experience. By contrast, to preach intertextually is to draw into prominence particular dimensions of the already existing web, and to make explicit the meaning-making connections, enabling others to search their own lives to do the same. It is the difference between play-acting and actually living.

• • •

In this book, we have raised to prominence one dimension of the intertextual web, that is, the relationship between faith and pop culture, and more specifically, preaching and the work of the band U2. In some sermons, we see how the music of U2 has profoundly shaped a reading of the biblical text. From the moment I first heard "Beautiful Day," I couldn't wait to preach on Noah. The two lines that allude to the Noah narrative demanded that I preach not on a narrow, individualistic notion of human sin, but on global issues of destruction and hope. For Jay Lawlor, Brian Walsh, and Jamie Howison, U2's music inspires a reading of the lament Psalms which draws out of them contemporary challenges to Pollyanna piety, to the church's worship, and to our complicity in injustice.

In other sermons, it is the Biblical text which has shaped the meanings found in U2's lyrics. Wade Hodges finds the grace that makes beauty in God's shout of blessing from the cross. Leslie Reinke sees the transformative power of Christ echoed in "Gone." And the Playboy Mansion becomes a shadow of the heavenly mansions of John 14 in Derek Walmsley's sermon.

And in still other sermons, the relationship is more subtle—U2 and the biblical text combine to call forth new meanings, new readings of other texts. From the doubt of "I Still Haven't Found What I'm Looking For" and the risk-filled action of Mary anointing Jesus emerges a new voice of faithful hope in Anna Carter Florence's sermon; for Henry VanderSpek, a visit to Deathclock.com pulls into view scripture after scripture and song after song, conspiring together to create a fragrant life from the fear of death.

This is no superficial borrowing from popular culture to attract or appease "the kids," nor is it a jettisoning of biblical tradition for the same purpose. Rather, it is a bringing into view the rich theological reflection which surrounds pop culture, a raising up of the meaning-making process that is constantly occurring as we engage in life and work out our faith.

So how do we do it? What steps can a preacher take to prepare a sermon that is richly intertextual and draws appropriately on popular culture alongside scripture?

First, listen. Listen prayerfully to the world around you. Saturate yourself in the articulations of our culture, whether in music, art, film, or TV. Be attentive to connections and allusions, both explicit and implicit. Wonder whether Tyne Daly's character cutting her hair at the end of an episode of *Judging Amy* has anything to do with biblical patterns of mourning. Find out what Martin Sheen's President Bartlet is saying when he rails at God in a darkened National Cathedral. Hunt out biblical allusions in the speeches of our politicians and military leaders. Read poetry, and look for the depths of human experience. Turn on the radio or VH-1, and hear what is heard by hundreds of thousands of people. Pay attention to where God might be active.

Listen prayerfully to your self. Allow your mind to wander, and keep track of its wanderings. Take note of the songs you just can't get out of your head, the images seared on your mind.

Listen prayerfully to the text. Read it, first, not for understanding but for God's word to you. Just as the body of a beloved one becomes a cadaver under the scalpel of a forensic pathologist, so too God's words can become devoid of life if we only approach them with an exegetical scalpel. When you approach the biblical text, bring your other listenings with you. Don't shut them out of the process of interpretation, but be aware of how they influence your reactions to the text, how they push you in one direction rather than another. In the beginning, this process of listening is something we need to do consciously. Over time, as the habit of listening becomes ingrained, it will occur naturally.

And then, as you begin your exegetical work, keep all those listenings in mind. Write down the connections, the obscure things which leap to mind as you read commentaries, as you struggle with the Greek and Hebrew. Don't worry if your page becomes filled with random jottings and lines cutting across each other. Just let it fill up with the intersections, the allusions, the bare threads of connection.

When it comes time to write the sermon, you will not need to hunt for illustrations on the Internet or conjure stories from thin air. It will all be there for you in that intertextual web. Pick up one thread, follow it carefully, and there you will find your sermon. And above all trust. Trust that your mind will do its work, and the Holy Spirit of God will do no less.

Does pop culture have anything to do with preaching? Absolutely! It expresses the longings, the doubts, the hopes, and the celebrations of the human spirit, the very same longings, doubts, hopes, and celebrations that are woven into Christian spirituality. Pop culture challenges religious practice, while simultaneously drawing upon the wealth of spiritual tradition. And it is a rich contributor to the incarnational "stuff" that sets preaching apart from learned lectures about abstract belief systems, that points us to a living, active God.

So in the words of U2's "Mofo," then, "Woo me, sister / Move me, brother"; preach the gospel of a God who lived and died among us and who dares to keep speaking the language of incarnate being, the language of love.

appendix B

A Brief History of U2 for Novices
Beth Maynard

The U2 story is a rich one and contains many more attractions and detours than are covered in the sermons in this book. Since there are any number of places to learn about U2's career for people who feel no special need to look at it through a theological lens, this chapter makes no attempt to write a generalist history of the band. However, for those (admittedly a much smaller number) who know theology but not U2, this essay may help to set Get Up Off Your Knees *in context. Here are the highlights of how the band has dealt with spiritual themes in its work.*

As one of the few bands that can be plausibly named in the same breath with greats like the Beatles or the Rolling Stones, U2 is anything but a "Christian rock group." They are simply artists who find it natural to draw on Biblical imagery and raise religious issues in their work. To put the issue in writers' terms, the analogue to U2 is not people whose works sit on the shelves of inspirational goods stores like *Left Behind* authors Tim LaHaye and Jerry Jenkins, but mainstream novelists like Flannery O'Connor, Anne Lamott, or John Updike. They wrestle with spiritual themes and set nuggets of Scripture in the midst of their work, but they compete in the marketplace rather than preach to the choir.

Just as literary critics do not typically pick over the minutiae of Updike's or O'Connor's work in efforts to deduce the authors' personal doctrines, there is little point for a book like this one to spend time asking, "What do the members of U2 actually believe?" Apart from being inappropriately voyeuristic, the question betrays a misunderstanding of how art works in the first place. However, a few words about their backgrounds may serve to set the stage.

U2's frontman Bono (real name Paul Hewson) attended an Anglican church as a child, but was marked most clearly by being the child of an exceptional (in Ireland) mixed Catholic/Protestant marriage. He also is said to have been impressed by the faith of a close friend's Plymouth Brethren family. David Evans (known as The Edge) came from a line of Welsh Presbyterians. Larry Mullen, Jr. had a traditional Roman Catholic upbringing, and Adam Clayton is from Protestant stock. This diverse mixture, sometimes jokingly spoken of as making the band "5/8 Protestant," surely set the stage for a spiritual commitment that did not sit easily with the institutional divisions of Christianity.

U2 formed in 1976, while the members were still in high school, and soon began getting gigs on a local scale. They released their first album, *Boy*, in 1980 and played some European and U.S. tour dates to promote it. During this formative era, Larry Mullen, the Edge, and Bono had become deeply involved in an intentional Christian community called Shalom, which was nondenominational and charismatic. The intense absorption in spiritual issues, the corporate ecstatic experience, and the Bible- and Jesus-centrism of that milieu were to mark them forever. The power of the experience can perhaps be judged by the fact that, when the community eventually challenged three-fourths of what was to become the top rock band in the world to renounce their musical vocation for fear it might hamper their spiritual growth, they nearly said yes.

While *Boy* had been mostly about the confusion and idealism of adolescence, their second album, *October* (1981), is the musical record of their vocational struggle, beginning with the glossolalic exhilaration of "Gloria" and ending with the poignant, self-doubting question, "Is that all? Is that all you want from me?" (Nearly every time I listen to it, I turn to the CD player and tell the singer, "Yes. Don't worry. That's all He wants from you.") *October* is a flawed work, evidencing the external pressure the band was under to produce more aggressively evangelistic material, but it also captures irresistibly the fervor and excess of the early years following a conversion.

Fortunately for posterity, the three Christian members of U2 did not make good on their intention to leave rock 'n' roll after the release of *October.* Instead they left Shalom. While continuing as believers, they would no longer, at least not publicly, accept any identification with an established Christian body. They settled a number of other issues around this time for good as well: They would not push their agnostic bandmate Adam Clayton to endorse their beliefs, turn interviews into opportunities for proselytizing, or put a religious agenda ahead of the integrity of their music. All of these choices, while earning them denunciations from some evangelicals, were to make possible a far wider sphere of influence for Christ than U2's critics dreamed.

U2's next album, *War* (1983), was no less spiritual, but introduced another major note that has consistently sounded in their work: social justice. The opening track, "Sunday Bloody Sunday," was a pacifist anthem responding to Catholic/Protestant violence in Northern Ireland, and more generally to the entire notion of violence as a solution to anything. In live performances of the song, Bono would march, waving a white flag, and entice audiences to chant, "No more! No war!"—a scene which older Generation Xers grew up seeing repeated ad infinitum on the fledgling cable channel MTV. Other tracks drew inspiration from the anti-nuclear movement, the Solidarity union in Poland, and the plight of refugees, often with subtle Biblical images interwoven throughout.

The Unforgettable Fire (1985) was a more experimental record, taking its title from a display about Hiroshima at the Chicago Peace Museum. Its standout tracks were "Pride," an anthem in praise of Martin Luther King, and "Bad," one of U2's anti-drug songs. In this mid-80s period, U2 was solidifying their reputation as above all a live band, able to build audience connections that led both musicians and participants into a kind of transcendence. Their international break came at the Live Aid benefit for Africa, when a passionate performance during which Bono leapt from the Wembley

Stadium stage riveted the attention of the world on what had been a B-level band. Soon after this broadcast, they were touring in support of Amnesty International and preparing for the release that would propel them into superstardom: 1987's *The Joshua Tree*. A perennial frontrunner in lists of the greatest rock albums, *The Joshua Tree* brought together themes and techniques with which U2 had been experimenting. It found the band in the American West, dressed like contemporary prophets and calling down the Spirit on a self-absorbed and frivolous decade. Listeners were riveted by the album's solemn ambiance, its recourse to the most basic Biblical images (thorns, nails, wind, locusts, deserts, mountains, fire, rain), and its nakedly honest aspiration for justice and the holy. *Time* magazine put U2 on its cover, in letters of flame, and proclaimed them Rock's Hottest Ticket.

If, in that era, you were a music fan, a believer, and at all susceptible to a blend of the Gospel and radical politics, *The Joshua Tree*'s highlights almost certainly became signposts on your spiritual map. The opener, "Where the Streets Have No Name," both evokes and mysteriously fulfills a longing for the ultimate; "Streets" has been a concert favorite ever since, developing live over the years into a moment of heavenly liberation in the middle of every U2 show, as the brightest light imaginable bursts forth from the stage to strike the audience momentarily blind. "I Still Haven't Found What I'm Looking For," a Gospel song, affirms in explicit terms faith in Christ and in the Atonement, but holds in mature tension the already/not yet that leaves redeemed Christians still yearning for the fullness of the Kingdom. "Bullet the Blue Sky" critiques Reagan-era U.S. intervention in Central America; "Running to Stand Still" explores addiction; "One Tree Hill" vows faith in the face of loss, combining elegiac lines about a friend (to whom the song is dedicated), and the martyred Chilean activist and folksinger Victor Jara, with a subtle evocation of end-time redemption and a wrenching wail to God to send the pentecostal Latter Rain.

As the 80s drew to a close, U2 was everywhere: TV, radio, print media, and in a thousand church basements as youth groups discussed tracks from the album. As buzz tipped into overexposure, their perceived seriousness and religiosity began to look to some like self-righteousness, and Bono in particular was much criticized for trying to save the world. After their overambitious film *Rattle and Hum* earned mixed reviews, the band announced that they were going away to "dream it all up again." It was widely thought this might mean that, just as the Beatles had broken up in 1970, U2 would die with the decade that had defined them.

What U2 did instead was reinvent themselves entirely as a band. They took their hearts off their sleeves and claimed a new identity as artists of irony. Moving away from sincere outpourings of hope and justice, they began to write about sex and betrayal. Instead of striving for transparency, they learned how to dissimulate and turn inquiries back on the questioner. Instead of their traditional minimalist stage with virtually no costuming, they explored the visual clichés of stardom in as excessive a fashion as they could muster.

Their first album of the 1990s, *Achtung Baby*, was brilliant, twisted, powerful—a total departure from their 80s style. And the mammoth tour that followed it, christened "ZooTV," blasted even more contradictions at the audience at a rate too fast to absorb. The word BELIEVE would fill the screens on the video wall, for example; then the outer letters would dissolve to leave only LIE. A blasé Bono zapped though TV channels rejecting substantial programming in search of something "rock 'n' roll enough"; audience members were brought onstage to film the goings-on; gaudy Trabant automobiles from the former Eastern bloc hung from the rafters and doubled as spotlights. What on earth was all this about?

But if you looked beneath the surface, the band was still pushing listeners to ask the deep questions. Depending on what Zoo-era concert you showed up for, you might find yourself greeted by The Disposable Heroes of Hiphoprisy rapping, "One nation under God has turned into one nation under the influence of one drug: Television." Or a chilling doctored clip of the first President Bush discussing the Gulf War ("I instructed our military commanders to totally rock Baghdad . . .") Or a sound loop asking again and again for your answer to the quintessentially religious question, "What do you want?"

Bono himself disappeared behind a leather-clad, amoral rock-star character named the Fly; he also performed as Mirrorball Man, a fanatical American televangelist in a *Joshua Tree* cowboy hat, and—borrowing a page from C. S. Lewis'

Screwtape Letters—as the devil himself, giving Satan's traditional name an Irish twist: MacPhisto. MacPhisto had a habit of making onstage calls to politicians, but one night he telephoned Archbishop of Canterbury George Carey, announcing that some of his best friends were religious leaders, and that the Church was doing a better job than the Evil One at alienating people from God.

Faded, pudgy, and decadent, MacPhisto came out for the encores, in which ZooTV's overload and indulgence was followed up with a subtle display of the wages of sin. Perhaps his most poignant speech was from the final Zoo show in Dublin, when U2's lifetime longing for God slipped out, refracted through the character's warped sadness: "There is someone who used to come and see us all the time; . . . we used to be so close. People think I've forgotten about him, but I haven't. . . . I was his most magnificent creation, the brightest star in his sky, and now look at me. . . .Who can I get to help me make peace with him? Who will mediate for me?"[7] Characteristic of U2 in the 1990s, if you wanted to know the answer to that, you would have to figure it out for yourself.

By the end of ZooTV, U2 had moved, in their own words, "from Psalms to Ecclesiastes."[8] 1993's *Zooropa*, released while the tour was still in progress, referenced the latter book's themes more than once in songs like "The First Time," "The Wanderer," and "Numb." But rather than turning around to head home at last, U2 continued down the road of experimentation with *Pop* (1997), which drew on mid-90s club and dance culture. The packaging was colorful, the title carefree, and the first video ("Discotheque") a campy, bizarre delight in which U2 actually dressed as the Village People. But after a few hearings, it was hard for a theologically-astute listener not to be struck by the bitter God-hauntedness of the songs. Many of the tracks were psalms of lament disguised as pulsing rave pieces.

"You want heaven in your heart, but you'll take what you can get if it's all that you can find." "God's got his phone off

7   Pimm Jal de la Parra, *U2 Live: A Concert Documentary* (New York: Omnibus Press, 1994), 170.

8   Bill Flanagan, *U2 at the End of the World* (New York: Delacorte Press, 1995; reprint; New York: Dell Publishing, 1996), 434.

the hook, babe; would he even pick up if he could?" And the album's dark final track, addressed to Christ, begs "tell me the story . . . about how it's all gonna be. . . . maybe your hands aren't free? . . . will you put a word in for me?" Its title? "Wake Up Dead Man." This was all material solidly in the Biblical tradition, but a long way from the ecstatic celebration of U2's early work.

ZooTV had confronted television culture; the Popmart tour took on another idol, consumerism, decorating stadiums all over the world with a giant McDonald's-style arch, a martini swizzle-stick complete with olive, and a 40-foot mirrorball lemon. Perhaps all this trashiness was meant to symbolize the quest spoken of in the show's opening song, "Mofo": "Looking for the baby Jesus under the trash." Still, the spectacle was not especially well received in America, although the rest of the world responded better; *Pop* was the band's least successful studio album.

Thus, at the end of their second decade as a collective, one reading of the story so far was that the U2 phenomenon just might have run its course. *Pop* had its boosters, but some listeners thought U2 had lost touch with what made them great. Others saw the band as slavishly trying to ride the coattails of new musical trends that were completely out of character for them. And the inevitable coterie of self-appointed religious judges theorized that U2 had finally ended a journey from genuine faith through questioning into spiritual death.

Strangely, even people who knew the story that the singer begged Jesus to tell in "Wake Up Dead Man" didn't, at the time, give much thought to what chapter comes after the one on death. However, resurrection language was in the air almost immediately when U2 finally released their first album of the new millennium, *All That You Can't Leave Behind.* (It had been delayed by Bono's frequent absence from the sessions because of his campaigning for third-world debt forgiveness as part of the Jubilee 2000 initiative.)

There were fewer explicit religious references on this work than on *Pop,* and several of the songs dealt with heavy themes like loss and death; nevertheless, the rebirth of hope was intoxicating. "Beautiful Day" celebrated the rainbow after the flood in a rapturous survey of creation; the irresistible God-and/or-sex rocker called "Elevation" opened with whoops of joy; "Walk On," dedicated to human rights activist Aung San

Suu Kyi, was an old-school U2 anthem which anyone in need of encouragement could appropriate. And the CD concluded with a pearl-like confession: "Grace removes the stain; grace makes beauty out of ugly things." When the material was combined with a very savvy promotional scheme, it was almost inevitable that *All That You Can't Leave Behind* would be hailed as U2's third masterpiece.

The Elevation Tour that followed in 2001 was back-to-basics: four guys on a stage with some lights and a sound system. A heart-shaped ramp let the band move amongst and encircle some of the audience; it was perhaps the most effective of their career-long efforts to break down the theatrical fourth wall (after all, what's the name of this band? You, too.). And even the old songs of joy were kicked up a notch. The early hit "I Will Follow" acquired a new crop of "Amazing Grace" references, and the eschatological barn-burner "Streets" got an extra Bible quote or two (among them an almost Eucharistic preface from Ps. 116:12–14). Where the band had once hoped to "take shelter" from the rain, now they vowed to "dance, dance, dance" in it.

Was this just 1987 redux, with idealistic/religious/save-the-planet U2 reprising their role as the biggest band in the world? The comparison is deceptive, because the Elevation Tour was not merely a return to old U2 habits. Everything that had changed them in the 90s was still there: the questioning spirit, the openness to experience, the fascination with the human propensity for sin. I remember some theology-minded friends trying to come up with a metaphor for this artistic process; there was only one that worked. "This could never have happened without their going through ZooTV and *Pop*. It's like when you tell a congregation if they really want to experience Easter, they have to come to the Holy Week services," one commented. Another was even briefer in her reference to the condition of Christ's risen, post-suffering body: "This new stuff," she said, "has a glorified-wounds thing going on."

Well, America in particular was soon to need someone who could promise us glorified wounds. In the wake of the terrorist attacks of September 11, 2001, U2 at first considered canceling the third leg of the Elevation Tour, which had been slated to return to America in October 2001. But as popular culture began to appropriate *All That You Can't Leave Behind* material as a way of working through grief, it became apparent how wise their decision to go through with that final set of dates was. U2 rose to the occasion and created a liturgy in the guise of a rock show, reworking their set list and their symbolism in a way that opened the event up to the Spirit, but never manipulated or lectured. New York firefighters were brought onstage at some dates; names of the victims of terrorism were projected; audience members wept and swayed as they sang along. Something extraordinary was happening. Bono kept talking about "God walking through the room" on the tour in a way that made U2 fans who had ridden through the late-80s backlash nervous,[9] but somehow the critics never really attacked this time. Apparently U2 had finally learned how to walk the fine line of celebrity, balancing their seriousness with self-mockery and their political-cum-spiritual commitment with rock star ridiculousness. Not only did the album shoot back up the charts, but the press began writing about the shows in a way that all but promised: Participate in this event and you will experience healing. Some people rolled their eyes, yes; a lot more, however, experienced healing.

Where U2 will head next remains to be seen; the only thing that is certain about a new U2 project is that it will be different from the old U2 projects. Given U2's propensity for continual self-reinvention, the medium will likely change again, the message will likely keep growing in maturity and nuance, and challenges to act for justice will never be far away. U2 is, after all, a band who knows deep down what their call is and isn't—whether they explicitly name it as their call or not.

To my mind, when the Spirit breaks through in a U2 show, when a text inspires a listener to confront ultimate questions, or when an anthem of longing lays bare someone's own "God-shaped hole," that is when U2 hit the peak of their vocation and, appropriately, get out of the way. They are an ideal pop culture example of someone's living out the vocation classically called *Praeparatio Evangelica*—raising questions and making connections that lay preliminary groundwork for the Gospel—and when they come to the edge of that task, they stop and step back. Yes, Someone else can take over, but

9   Chris Heath, "U2 Tour: From the Heart," *Rolling Stone* (May 10, 2001).

how much better if those of us who claim to work for Him were ready to step in, in an attitude of grace and servanthood, as well.

After all, one by-product of the 25-year history we've just covered is that a generation of concert-goers exists now—gathered not in church pews, but in Internet chat rooms and coffee houses—who have experienced God though this band, often with no religious vocabulary to express it. It's not U2's job to offer them that vocabulary. But if you are a preacher, I think it might be yours.

Pursuing God With U2:
An Adult Study

Beth Maynard

This is a six-week program on aspects of God in the music of U2 designed for adult spiritual formation groups. A couple of words up front about the structure and assumptions of the course may be helpful.

First, while this material simply assumes that contemporary popular media is a useful place to look for the footprints of the Holy Spirit, it does not assume that participants have a deep familiarity with U2. If you have fans in your group, however, by all means use them as resources; they will probably know much of what is given here as explanatory material.

Second, U2 is not a "Christian band," but some of its members are Christians with significant fluency in the vocabulary of the Christian tradition. Thus, throughout their work U2 naturally raises and wrestles with spiritual questions using that vocabulary. Like all art, the results have many levels of meaning and can be viewed from diverse perspectives, especially when you consider that U2's catalog spans more than two decades. This course skips around without giving much attention to which themes U2 emphasized when, and of course highlights only a few of many possible readings of the music.

Third, this course intentionally uses what, in many church settings, will probably seem to be a large quantity of visual and auditory media, allowing much of it to stand without editorial comment or interpretation. While this may be uncomfortable to persons accustomed to a linear or text-based classroom style, people of the ages U2 tends to attract naturally absorb media without requiring propositional statements claiming to encapsulate its "real meaning." Thus, the sessions' use of media is designed to make the structure of the course itself instructive, in a subtle way, for more traditional church groups.

Thus, you're urged not to cut the opening, closing, and background music, and you're urged to find as much of this material as you possibly can. The course cannot be put on by handing out lyric sheets. There are a few must-have items, and then additional possibilities for those who have access to more material. All the items listed are available both used and new through CD and video stores or rental outlets, as well as through internet book, media, and auction sites. In all cases, the track information refers to American releases. The class will flow much more smoothly if you recruit a second person to be responsible for cuing up and starting video and audio rather than trying to do it yourself.

To offer this course you need the following:
On CD: *The Joshua Tree; All That You Can't Leave Behind; War*
On DVD: *Elevation 2001: Live From Boston;*
The Best of 1990–2000
Recommended on CD: *Pop; The Best of 1980–1990*
Additional possibilities:
On CD: *Achtung Baby; Boy*
On VHS: *The Best of 1980–1990* or *Under a Blood Red Sky*

Approximate running times are given for each section of the class. The minimum time needed for each session is 50 minutes at a brisk pace; 75 or 90 would make for a better experience.

session 1

Pursuing God as Ultimate

*As people arrive, play "I Still Haven't Found What I'm Looking For" (*The Joshua Tree *CD)*

Introduction: 10 minutes
Begin with a prayer. Cover any ground rules you want to set for the class. Then using the essay in this book or your own knowledge, give (or if your class contains U2 fans, draw out of them with questions) brief historical background on U2. Make sure to explain that they are not an example of "Christian rock," but a mainstream band, and to point out that their brand of faith is not one that has sat easily with the institutional aspect of Christianity. Comment on why you've chosen to offer a class on their work.

For our first session, we're going to focus on one live performance video from the year 2001. The song dates from 1987, but it has been a highlight of live U2 concerts since then.

Hand out lyrics to "Where the Streets Have No Name" and give people a chance to read them.

Very quickly, on a surface level, what does this song seem to be about?
 • *desire for an ideal place*
 • *escape*
 • *freedom from dividing labels ["no name"]*
 • *transcendence of negative things ["dust cloud," "poison rain"]*

Video and Discussion: 15–20 minutes
*Watch "Streets" (*Elevation 2001: Live From Boston *DVD, 6:43) Be aware that there are some lyric changes in this live performance.*

We're coming in at the apex of the concert, transitioning out of a song about addictions into "Streets," the one we're going to focus on. You'll hear Bono recite a prayer based on Psalm 116:12-14 during the introduction, then move into the actual song, and as you watch I want to give you a few things to look for:

- Observe the use of light
- Listen for the crowd singing along (easiest to hear at the beginning); they are singing at the top of their lungs, but are low in the mix
- If you know a Christian tradition that uses physical gestures in worship, watch for any that may be familiar to you
- Note how the band behaves at the "curtain call" moment at the end

Large group discussion questions:

1. What did you notice?

Take answers, putting them on newsprint if you care to, and invite reflections on what these things convey. Possible answers include:

- *use of light: shimmering effect at beginning and end, blinding bursts of white/gold light during the song, use of the color red*
- *gesture: orans position/hands raised, kneeling/genuflecting, eyes closed, peace sign, prayer posture of hands at end, "God bless you"*

2. What did you feel as you watched?

3. Is what we've just seen a worship event? What evidence supports your answer?

Small Groups: 10–20 minutes

Break into groups of no more than 4 and ask them to discuss as many of the following questions as you have time for. Play tracks 1–3 of The Joshua Tree *CD quietly in the background.*

1. When in your life, in any context, have you felt like what we just watched?

2. C. S. Lewis writes that if we are designed for connection with God, for heaven, that the longing for that connection will be felt in us like a desire "for our proper place . . . for our own far-off country . . . for something that has never actually appeared in our experience."[10] If we take this song as voicing such a desire, a longing for direct encounter with God, what is your reaction to the intensity we saw on the video? Why?

- I identify; I've been there
- I wish I could experience that kind of thing
- That kind of desire for God might come a few times in someone's life, but it's not normal or sustainable
- Seeing that kind of passion about spiritual things makes me nervous because . . .
- I don't buy Lewis' statement, or I don't buy that what we see on the video has anything to do with spirituality
- Other

3. The lyrics to the song say, "And when I go there, I go there with you." At the end, the band is seen clapping for their audience. What does this say about the role of community in connecting with God? When have you experienced a corporate connection with God that inspired you?

Large Group Conclusion: 10–15 minutes
Discussion questions:
1. Imagine that you were part of the event on the video. If you were using those 7 minutes as information about what God is like, what conclusions would you draw?

2. Compare and contrast this with at least one other event you've experienced that purported to show what God is like. (You might want to make a list with two columns.) What are the pros and cons of each?

---

10 C. S. Lewis, *The Weight of Glory and Other Addresses,* revised and expanded edition (New York: Macmillan, 1980), 6-7.

Closing: 5 minutes
Give an overview of what's coming next; cover any housekeeping issues.

Prayer Time:
Pray in whatever fashion is most native to your group, or call the group to prayer, then read again the first stanza of the lyrics to "Streets."

Ask: If you were writing a song like this right now, about what your deepest longing in life is, how would it begin? Silently *(or aloud, depending on the tolerance of your group)* tell God, "I want to . . . ." *Then close with Rev. 22:17:* "The Spirit and the bride say, 'Come.' And let everyone who hears say, 'Come.' And let everyone who is thirsty come. Let anyone who wishes take the water of life as a gift."

Outro:
Before talking begins, immediately put on "40" (War CD) as people are getting up to go.

Pursuing God as Justice

As people arrive, play "Mothers of the Disappeared" (The Joshua Tree CD)

Introduction: 2–3 minutes
Pray; cover any announcements; introduce topic of this session.

Video and Discussion: 15–20 minutes
Explain, or draw out of fans in your group: U2 is from the Republic of Ireland. This 1983 song is about sectarian violence in Northern Ireland, but has also been applied to many other situations of evil. We're not looking so much for specific visuals this time as for the general feel of the song, and I'd like you to follow the lyrics as we watch.

Hand out lyrics; play "Sunday Bloody Sunday" (ideally watch a performance from the early 80s on The Best of 1980–1990 *VHS or the* Under A Blood Red Sky *VHS (these two are identical—approximately 6:00); or play the studio version from* War *(4:40); if you have extra time, it's also available on the* Elevation 2001: Live From Boston *DVD (8:04).*

Large group discussion questions:
(write answers up on newsprint if you care to)

1. What are some of the striking images to you in this song?
   - *how long*
   - *broken bottles*
   - *bodies strewn across a dead end street*
   - *battle call*
   - *trenches*

2. Where do you find hope in the text?
- *"Tonight we can be as one"*
- *"Wipe your tears away"*
- *"Claim the victory Jesus won"*

3. What does it call the listener to? A pacifist response? Outrage? Turning to Jesus? Wiping others' tears?

Small Groups: 10–20 minutes
Break into groups of no more than four. Ask them to discuss as many of the following questions as you have time for. During it, play the War CD beginning with track 1 quietly in the background.

1. What situations in the world right now leave you saying "How long?"

2. When I hear the image of being "immune," numbed by the amount of suffering covered on TV, I. . .
- know exactly what it means; one person can't do anything to help
- know what it means but just pray God will change things
- understand, but deal with it by choosing a few causes where I know I can make a difference
- don't relate; even when it's far away, I feel very strongly for suffering and get involved
- think those people should be solving their own problems
- other

3. What do you think is meant by "the victory Jesus won on a Sunday Bloody Sunday?" If you believe in this victory, explain what you think it offers in situations of hunger, oppression, or violence. If you don't, give your reaction to people's comments.

Large Group Conclusion: 15–25 minutes
Get volunteers to read the following two quotations:

Such fasting as you do today
will not make your voice heard on high.
Is such the fast that I choose, a day to humble oneself?

Is it to bow down the head like a bulrush,
and to lie in sackcloth and ashes?
Will you call this a fast, a day acceptable to the Lord?
Is not this the fast that I choose:
to loose the bonds of injustice,
to undo the thongs of the yoke,
to let the oppressed go free, and to break every yoke?
Is it not to share your bread with the hungry,
and bring the homeless poor into your house;
when you see the naked, to cover them,
and not to hide yourself from your own kin?
(Isa. 58: 4–7)

> There is a radical side to Christianity that I am attracted to. And I think without a commitment to social justice, it is empty. Are they putting money into AIDS research? Are they investing in hospitals so the lame can walk? So the blind can see? . . . If you are not committed to the poor, what is religion? It's a black hole.[11]

Discussion questions:
(as many as you have time for)

1. What do these quotations have in common?

2. Do you agree that without a commitment to social justice, Christianity is empty? Why or why not?

3. List some other important parts of discipleship. How does social justice relate to them?

4. Whatever you may think about specific social issues, why is it important that Christians act out the love and compassion they preach?

5. Is there a specific situation on which our group could agree to take action together?

---

11 David Breskin, "Bono: U2's Passionate Voice," *Rolling Stone*, October 8, 1987.

Closing: 7–10 minutes
Give an overview of what's coming next; cover any housekeeping issues.

We're going to finish by watching a video from the late 90s which specifically calls people who claim to have a relationship with God to take action. Watch for how that call is made, and for how many different kinds of people are part of the world it imagines.
*Watch the video "Please" together (*The Best of 1990–2000 *DVD, 5:02)*

Prayer Time:
After "Please" ends, without commenting on it, offer a very brief prayer and dismiss the group.

Outro:
As people are leaving, put on "Peace on Earth" from the All That You Can't Leave Behind *CD.*

session 3

Pursuing God as Absent

As people arrive, play "With or Without You" (The Joshua Tree CD; also available on The Best of 1980–1990 *CD or VHS)*

Introduction: 2–3 minutes
Pray; cover any announcements; introduce the topic of this session.

Song and Discussion: 15–20 minutes
There are a lot of places in Scripture where people express anger at God and accuse God of being too absent from the world, especially in the Psalms. This is a theme U2 has picked up on frequently. We're going to look first at a Biblical Psalm, and then at the contemporary one with which U2 ended the 1997 album *Pop.*

Have a volunteer read:

> Hear my prayer, O Lord;
> give ear to my supplications in your faithfulness;
> answer me in your righteousness.
> Do not enter into judgment with your servant,
> for no one living is righteous before you.
>
> For the enemy has pursued me,
> crushing my life to the ground,
> making me sit in darkness like those long dead.
> Therefore my spirit faints within me;
> my heart within me is appalled.
>
> I remember the days of old,
> I think about all your deeds,
> I meditate on the works of your hands.

I stretch out my hands to you;
my soul thirsts for you like a parched land.

Answer me quickly, O Lord;
my spirit fails.
Do not hide your face from me,
or I shall be like those who go down to the Pit.
Let me hear of your steadfast love in the morning,
for in you I put my trust." (Ps. 143:1–8)

1. What is the Psalmist's complaint about his condition and the condition of the world?

2. What is he remembering as he suffers?

3. What does he hope for?

4. Let's compare the voice of the Psalmist to the voice that speaks in a U2 song.

Hand out the lyrics to "Wake Up Dead Man." If you have the album Pop, *listen to the song and follow the lyrics (4:52); if not, watch it on the* Elevation 2001: Live From Boston *DVD (1:22)—but be aware that the entire text is not performed there because it segues immediately into another song.*

Large group discussion questions:
1. What is your reaction to this song?

2. How is it similar to or different than the Psalm?
   Possible differences:
   - *the song explicitly addresses Jesus*
   - *raises the issue that God's hands may be tied in some situations*
   - *there's nothing like the "listen" section in the Psalm*

   Possible similarities
   - *mood of despair, honesty*
   - *sense of God's absence*
   - *setting suffering in the context of faith*
   - *both want to be reminded of God's past story*

3. Do you think there is one speaker in this song, or two? If two, which parts are addressed to whom?
People who perceive two speakers often say the "listen" section is addressed back to the main speaker by Jesus. Some also think Jesus speaks the line "wake up dead man." Others think there is one speaker only.

4. How would you describe the Jesus of this song?
Powerless? Compassionate? Trustworthy? Beyond human understanding? Disappointing but inescapable?

Small Groups: 10–15 minutes
Break into groups of no more than four and ask them to discuss as many of the following questions as you have time for. During it, play tracks 5–7 of Pop, *or if you do not have* Pop, *tracks 8–10 of the* All That You Can't Leave Behind *CD quietly in the background.*

1. Tell about one time when you felt like God was missing in action.

2. I think complaining to God when we feel alone and over-whelmed by the evil in the world. . .
  • is disrespectful to God
  • may help us feel better, but has no other effect
  • is a superstitious waste of God's time
  • is an important way of being honest with God
  • is part of how God changes the evil in the world
  • other

Individual Activity: 10–15 minutes
Using the Psalm and the lyrics as examples, write your own prayer of lament to God either voicing some concern you feel, or taking on the voice of someone in a specific situation of suffering known to you. You will not be asked to share these, so you can be completely open.

Large Group Conclusion: 7–8 minutes
We're going to finish by watching a video from the same album as "Wake Up Dead Man." This song expresses the same sort of idea, but I think you'll find that the mood is more tender and empathetic. Notice how the images of the video suggest that we are so involved in the pace of ordinary

life that we might miss God's presence even if it was with us. *Watch "If God Will Send His Angels"* (The Best of 1990–2000 DVD, 5:22).

Closing: 5 minutes
Give an overview of what's coming next; cover any housekeeping issues.

Prayer Time:
Close in prayer either extemporaneously or through inviting people to call out names and situations to which they wish God would "send his angels."

Outro:
As people leave, either play "Love is Blindness" (Achtung Baby CD,) *or re-play "With or Without You"* (The Joshua Tree CD) *or "Peace on Earth"* (All That You Can't Leave Behind CD.)

Pursuing God-Substitutes

*As people arrive, play "Running to Stand Still" (*The Joshua Tree CD)

Introduction: 2–3 minutes
Pray, cover any announcements, introduce topic of this session.

Videos and Discussion: 25–35 minutes
We're going to begin immediately with a Scripture reading. It takes place when Moses is up on Mount Sinai and the people decide they'd rather have a god who is a little easier to find than Yahweh seems to be.

Have a volunteer read:
> When the people saw that Moses delayed to come down from the mountain, the people gathered around Aaron, and said to him, "Come, make gods for us, who shall go before us; as for this Moses, the man who brought us up out of the land of Egypt, we do not know what has become of him." Aaron said to them, "Take off the gold rings that are on the ears of your wives, your sons, and your daughters, and bring them to me." So all the people took off the gold rings from their ears, and brought them to Aaron. He took the gold from them, formed it in a mold, and cast an image of a calf; and they said, "These are your gods, O Israel, who brought you up out of the land of Egypt!" When Aaron saw this, he built an altar before it; and Aaron made proclamation and said, "Tomorrow shall be a festival to the Lord." They rose early the next day, and offered burnt offerings and brought sacrifices of well-being; and the people sat down to eat and drink, and rose up to revel. (Ex. 32:1-6)

With no verbal comment at all, immediately start the video "Discothèque." (The Best of 1990–2000 DVD, 5:19)

1. What did you see in the video that connected with the reading?
People will probably just say: a lot of reveling. In fact, there's a much deeper connection.
Explain, or draw out of fans in your group: One of U2's artistic preoccupations is the allure and danger of addiction; some of their best-known songs are anti-drug songs. However, in their work drugs also represent something larger: anything we try to substitute for God's love. The philosopher Blaise Pascal put it this way: "We try in vain to fill the emptiness with everything around us, always looking for new things to try that we think might help us. But it never works, because this infinite abyss can only be filled with something that is infinite and unchanging—in other words, by God himself."[12]
When U2 was asked what the piece we've just seen was about, and specifically whether it was about drugs, Bono replied, "I think it's an earnest little riddle about love. . . .It's about the counterfeit of what you can't find. People take second best . . . it's not just drugs. There's lots of counterfeits out there."[13]

Hand out the lyrics and give people a chance to read them.

2. What statements does "Discothèque" make about the "real thing"?
   • *you can't grab it, control it, direct it*
   • *it's not a trick*
   • *it's the way*
   • *you can't earn it*

3. What does it say about the counterfeits?
   • *you know they're fake but want them anyway*
   • *you take what you can get*

12 Blaise Pascal, *Pensees*, section VII, pensee 425, paraphrase by the author.
13 Keith Cameron, "'...Only Now Do We Look Cool' (Part 1)," *NME*, March 8, 1997.

"Discothèque" highlights the temporary thrills of "bubblegum," the pleasures and distractions we substitute for God. We're now going to watch a very different video from 1993 which portrays the emptiness of a person who has sampled every possible God-substitute, and come out numbed and bored by the onslaught of experience.

Explain, or draw out of fans in your group: "Numb" comes from a period in U2's work where they were especially concerned about the anesthetizing effect of the media, so the flickering light you see in front represents a TV into which guitarist the Edge stares as he monotones hollow advice. It has a serious point, but you're allowed to laugh at it.

(Don't hand out lyrics for this one; the point is the visual.)
*Show the video "Numb" (Godley version) (*The Best of 1990–2000 DVD, 4:18*)*

1. What examples of pleasures, experiences, "bubblegum" did you see?
Sex of many kinds, food, smoking, TV, fame [fans taking pictures], acclaim [roses]

2. Could you tell what the high voice was saying? How does that fit in?
"Too much is not enough"—double meaning of the unending desire for more, along with the knowledge that it cannot satisfy

3. What do you make of the image of the singer getting tied up during all this?
Perhaps a visual allusion to the idea that "too much" inevitably enslaves

Small Groups: 10–15 minutes
Break into groups of no more than four and ask them to discuss as many of the following questions as you have time for. During it, play tracks 1–3 of Pop, *tracks 9–11 of* Achtung Baby, *or if you have neither of these, put on* The Best of 1990-2000 DVD *beginning from "Discothèque" again.*

1. What things have you seen that have this numbing effect on other people?
  - *alcohol or drugs*
  - *Internet use*
  - *workaholism*
  - *pace of life*
  - *money*
  - *prestige*
  - *pornography or sexual addiction*
  - *gambling*
  - *other*

2. What are you most likely to use to numb yourself? What are the counterfeits of God that you turn to most frequently?

3. How do you decide if a particular counterfeit is getting too much of a hold on you?

Large Group Closing: 5 minutes
Give an overview of what's coming next; cover any housekeeping issues.

Prayer Time:
Close in prayer using this quote from St. Augustine: "You have made us for yourself, O God, and our hearts are restless till they find rest in You."

Outro:
*As people leave, play either "Bad" (*The Best of 1980–1990 *CD or* Elevation 2001: Live From Boston *DVD), or "Surrender" (*War *CD).*

Pursuing God as Pursuer

As people arrive, play "When I Look at the World" (All That You Can't Leave Behind CD)

Introduction: 2–3 minutes
Pray; cover any announcements; introduce topic of this session.

Song, Video, and Discussion: 25–35 minutes
Some of you may know the classic children's story *The Runaway Bunny* by Margaret Wise Brown. *Ask if anyone can retell its basic point. For reference, the story begins:*

> Once there was a little bunny who wanted to run away, so he said to his mother, "I am running away."
>
> "If you run away," said his mother, "I will run after you. For you are my little bunny."
>
> "If you run after me," said the little bunny, "I will become a fish in a trout stream and I will swim away from you."
>
> "If you become a fish in a trout stream," said his mother, "I will become a fisherman and I will fish for you."[14]

Finally, when the bunny becomes convinced he cannot escape, he gives up on running away.

This story has comforted generations of children with the idea that Mom will never let them go. It has also been seen,

---

14 Margaret Wise Brown, *The Runaway Bunny* (New York: Harper & Row, Publishers, Inc., 1942. Revised edition, HarperCollins Children's Books, 1972), 1–3.

notably in Margaret Edson's play *Wit*, as an allegory of God's relentless pursuit of the human soul.

Explain, or draw out of fans in your group: U2 expresses basically the same idea in one of their earliest hits, "I Will Follow"; they were in their late teens when they wrote it. *(Hand out lyrics.)* The music has an almost stalker-like drive to it; the lyrics are, though intense, quite simplistic. Like many of Bono's lyrics, they blend the image of reconnecting with his mother (who died suddenly when he was 14) with the image of spiritual salvation. As you listen, try and think about who the pronouns I, you, they, and he refer to, and watch for quotations from a famous hymn.

Play "I Will Follow," ideally the studio version on either The Best of 1980–1990 *CD or* Boy, *3:36. If you do not have either, it appears in a more mellow version on the* Elevation 2001: Live From Boston *DVD, 5:10. If you are using the latter, be aware that there are lyric changes and that "Paradise" is the name of a club in Boston where U2 played on their first American tour.*

Large group discussion questions:

1. What was the hymn?
"Amazing Grace"

2. What could make you think this song is about following/stalking? What could make you think it's about being followed/stalked? Do you think it's about either, or both?
The question turns on who the "I" and "you" are and who is speaking when. Perhaps the entire song is spoken by the singer to someone else—Jesus? mother? lover? audience?—or vice versa; or perhaps the chorus is spoken by someone different, or by two people at once. There is no single, correct answer.

3. List some situations, good or bad, where the vow "if you walk away, I walk away; I will follow" might be made.
List answers on newsprint if you care to.

4. Do you think God makes this vow to us?

5. Let's look at an even stronger example. We will be returning to this song next week for its lyrical content, but tonight we're mostly going to concentrate on the staging.

Explain, or draw out of fans in your group: The text is sung by Judas to Jesus in the afterlife; at the end, as staged, he seems to repent, and Jesus seems to claim him. As you watch this, focus specifically on the last half's interaction between the singer Bono who is (more or less) playing Judas and the guitarist Edge who is (more or less) playing Jesus.

Play "Until the End of the World" (Elevation 2001: Live From Boston DVD, 5:18; the version on the Best of 1990–2000 *is not useful here.)*
(There is a lot of disorienting camera action, so after the first two verses, remind them to pay special attention to the singer and guitarist. During the guitar solo, point out Judas's kiss of betrayal.)

6. Again, we'll be looking at the text next week, but for now, what stood out to you most about this staging?
 • *looks like a battle or bullfight*
 • *intense, personal*
 • *Jesus wins*
 • *Judas's bravado*
 • *Judas resists, but stretches his arm out at the*
   very end

7. What would you say to this as an image of what encountering God is like?

Small Groups: 10–15 minutes
Break into groups of no more than four and ask them to discuss as many of the following questions as you have time for. During it, play the Boy *CD beginning with track 7, or if you do not have* Boy, The Joshua Tree *CD beginning with track 8.*

1. Vincent Donovan wrote a book about his work with the Masai of East Africa. In it, a Masai elder comments that his people tried to approach God as if they were lions stalking their prey, but after coming to faith they realized they were not the ones doing the stalking. "We have not searched for him. He has searched for us. He has searched us out and

found us. All the time we think we are the lion. In the end, the lion is God."[15]

I find the idea that God is searching for us with the intensity of a mother seeking a child or a lion stalking prey. . .
- comforting: God is all-powerful and will never let me wander away from his love.
- intimidating: I'm not sure I want to be stalked and captured by God.
- unrealistic: Surely God has more important things to worry about than me.
- other

2. Have you had an experience where you felt like God took the initiative with you? If so, and you are willing, share it with your group.

3. On a scale of 1 to 10, rate the intensity of you pursuit of God right now.
On a scale of 1 to 10, rate the intensity of God's pursuit of you right now.

Large Group Closing: 5–10 minutes
Give an overview of what's coming next; cover any housekeeping issues.

Prayer Time:
If your group is shy, you may wish to let them answer question number 3 above in silent prayer. To close, either pray by yourself, or have everyone pray together, this Psalm text:

> O Lord, you have searched me and known me.
> You know when I sit down and when I rise up;
> you discern my thoughts from far away.
> You search out my path and my lying down,
> and are acquainted with all my ways.
> Even before a word is on my tongue,

---

15 Vincent Donovan, *Christianity Rediscovered,* (Maryknoll, New York: Orbis Books, 1983), 63

O Lord, you know it completely.
You hem me in, behind and before,
and lay your hand upon me.
Such knowledge is too wonderful for me;
it is so high that I cannot attain it.

Where can I go from your spirit?
Or where can I flee from your presence?
If I ascend to heaven, you are there;
if I make my bed in Sheol, you are there.
If I take the wings of the morning
and settle at the farthest limits of the sea,
even there your hand shall lead me,
and your right hand shall hold me fast. (Ps.139:1–10)

Outro:
Before conversation begins, start playing "Drowning Man" (War CD) as people leave.

Pursuing God as Lover

As people arrive, if you have The Best of 1980-1990 *CD, play "All I Want is You." If not, play "In A Little While" (*All That You Can't Leave Behind *CD.)*

Introduction: 5 minutes
Cover any announcements, then introduce the topic of this session with the following prayer adapted from St. Augustine:

> My God, let me know and love you, so that I may find my happiness in you. Enable me to know you ever more on earth, so that I may know you perfectly in heaven. Enable me to love you ever more on earth, so that I may love you perfectly in heaven. O God of truth, grant me the happiness of heaven so that my joy may be full, in accord with your promise. In the meantime let my mind dwell on that happiness, my tongue speak of it, my heart pine for it, my mouth pronounce it, my soul hunger for it, my flesh thirst for it, and my entire being desire it until I enter through death into the joy of my Lord forever. Amen.

Large Group Videos and Discussion: 20–35 minutes
This prayer uses very sensual language and fits in with a long history of thinking of God as a lover or spouse within Christianity. For example, in Hosea 2, God says of his people: "I will now allure her, and bring her into the wilderness, and speak tenderly to her. . . . There she shall respond as in the days of her youth . . . . On that day, says the Lord, you will call me, 'My husband.'" Unlike much of the institutional church, U2 does not seem at all frightened of this image; they've used it since the early 80s. We're going to look at two examples, the

first being another version of something we watched last week.

Hand out lyrics to "Until the End of the World" and give people a chance to read them.
1. The words are spoken by Judas in the afterlife—what evidence do you see of that?
   • *description of Last Supper*
   • *took the money*
   • *in the garden*
   • *kissed your lips*

2. What romantic images do you see?
   • *close as bride and groom*
   • *led me on*
   • *playing the tart*
   • *kissed your lips and broke your heart*

We saw last week a depiction of the meeting between Jesus and Judas after the text ends; this week let's look at an earlier performance.

Play "Until the End of the World" (the version on The Best of 1990–2000 *DVD, 5:15. Feel free to cue it up after the opening newscaster portion, which is not relevant for this session.)*

3. What overall effect does this piece have on you?

That song centers around male images; there is also a long history of female images for God and especially the Holy Spirit. U2 picks up on that tradition frequently, and this love song to the Holy Spirit is one of their best known.

*Play the "Mysterious Ways" video (*The Best of 1990–2000 *DVD, 4:04.)*

4. What images do you see here that evoke the mystery and uncontrollable nature of the Spirit?
   • *mirror distortion effect*
   • *veils*
   • *setting in Morocco*
   • *belly dancer*

- *spinning*
- *unusual perspectives*

Explain, or draw out of fans in your group: When U2 were first performing this song live, they would push the visual pun a little further by having an actual belly dancer involved; she would approach the singer on stage but always remain just out of reach.

Hand out the lyrics and let people read through them.

5. Here the sexuality is more in the music and the visuals than in the lyrics, but are there particular lines that strike anyone?

6. What overall effect does this piece have on you?

Small Groups: 10–15 minutes
Break into groups of no more than four and ask them to discuss as many of the following questions as you have time for. During it, play the Elevation 2001: Live From Boston *DVD from the beginning.*

1. What is your reaction to evoking sexuality and God in the same breath?
- it's great; I think this way all the time
- it's new to me but I like it; I hope to explore this further
- it makes me a little uncomfortable, but I see the point
- I think it's in bad taste
- I think it's dangerous
- I'm not sure whether it's a good idea or not
- other

2. What visual or verbal image from either of the two videos connected most directly with your own experience of God?

Large Group Closing: 10–15 minutes
Review the topics the course has covered, and invite people to share in a sentence or two something that was meaningful to them or that they learned from participating in this group. (If you have more than about 20 in the class, ask this question in the small groups.)

Prayer Time:
Pray in thanksgiving, gathering up comments and learnings from the entire course. Dismiss everyone with a blessing.

Outro:
As people leave, play "Grace" (All That You Can't Leave Behind CD)

Contributors

Julie Bogart

Julie is an avid U2 fan. She credits Bono and his lyrics with breathing new life into her faith. Julie is also a contributing editor to *Worship Leader* magazine and runs an online writing business (www.bravewriter.com). In addition, she hosts an Internet forum called The Trapdoor Society (www.trapdoorsociety.com), which exists to promote a woman's self-education. Julie lives with her husband, Jon, and homeschools their five children in Cincinnati, Ohio.

Sarah Dylan Breuer

Dylan is a theologian, writer, and educator with a master's degree in New Testament from the University of St. Andrews in Scotland and a C. Phil. in the history of early Christianity from the University of California at Los Angeles (U.C.L.A.). She is also a singer-songwriter-guitarist who cut her hair just like Bono's in 1983, when she was 13, and who uses U2 music when teaching college classes on religion. Dylan serves as Director of Christian Formation at St. Martin's-in-the-Field Episcopal Church in Severna Park, Maryland, and she thanks Karen for elevation and inspiration.

Anna Carter Florence

Anna is assistant professor of preaching at Columbia Theological Seminary in Decatur, Georgia. An ordained minister in the Presbyterian Church (USA), she has focused much of her work on two of her passions: youth and poetics. She holds degrees from Yale College and Princeton Theological Seminary, has preached and lectured widely, and published numerous sermons and articles. Her book, *Preaching as Testimony,* is forthcoming from Westminster John Knox Press. Anna loves teaching and preaching in the South but is glad to return home to New England every summer so her two sons remember how to swim in cold water and pronounce the letter "R."

David Friedrich

Born in 1975, David holds a Bachelor of Music degree in classical guitar performance. He is currently a student at Harvard Divinity School, pursuing a Master of Divinity, and is also a youth minister at an Episcopal church in Massachusetts. The connections between pop culture and Christianity are vital to his ministry.

Steven Garber

Steven Garber has lived his life among students, and he speaks widely to professors as well as students on the relation of learning to life. A Senior Fellow with the Clapham Institute, he is also Fellow and Lilly Faculty Scholar at Calvin College. For many years a member of the faculty of the American Studies Program, an interdisciplinary semester of study on Capitol Hill, he is the author of *The Fabric of Faithfulness: Weaving Together Belief and Behavior During the University Years.* He served as the scholar-in-residence for the Council for Christian Colleges and Universities for several years, and continues on as a Senior Fellow for the C. S. Lewis Institute in Washington, D. C. A native of the great valleys of Colorado and California, he is married to Meg and with their five children lives in Virginia where they are members of The Falls Church.

Wade Hodges

Wade lives in Tulsa, Oklahoma with his wife, Heather, and their two sons, Caleb and Elijah. He is the Preaching Minister for the Garnett Church of Christ. When he's not preaching, Wade hikes beautiful trails, skis down treacherous mountains, makes solid wood furniture, and drinks an occasional cup of Starbucks coffee. He holds degrees in Communication and Christian Ministry from Abilene Christian University. His favorite part of sermon preparation is going to the movies. You can read his blog at www.wadehodges.com.

Jamie Howison

Jamie is a priest of the Anglican Church of Canada, currently serving as Pastor of the ground-breaking joint Anglican and Lutheran parish, The Church of St. Stephen & St. Bede in Winnipeg, Manitoba. He also serves as a teacher and trustee with an ecumenical GenX ministry called "Hear the Music," and as an occasional instructor with the Canadian Mennonite University's School of Discipleship. He believes that much of our best theology is done in the forms of music and literature, and his library of books and CDs is a noble attempt to defend that theory.

Mike Kinman

Mike is the Episcopal Chaplain at Washington University in St Louis, Missouri. He is a co-founder of Gathering the neXt Generation and works extensively with Christian community formation and leadership development among young adults. His love of U2 dates back to his college days in the mid-1980s, and he regularly uses their music and message in preaching, teaching and liturgy on campus.

Jay R. Lawlor

Jay is an Episcopal priest who has been a U2 fan since his early teens. He uses U2 material in sermons, Bible study, and in developing contemporary worship services for youth and young adults. Author of the book *The Church and International Development,* Jay trained as an economist and is especially interested in drawing attention to the social justice messages found in so many of U2's songs. He is currently Assistant Rector at Grace Episcopal Church in New Bedford, Massachusetts, and lives in New Bedford with his wife Angela.

Amy Lincoln

Amy is Associate Pastor for Family Ministry at Hilltop Church in Mendham, New Jersey. She grew up in Tampa, where her parents still live, and graduated in 1993 from Presbyterian College in Clinton, South Carolina, where she was an English major and a psychology minor. She spent her summer vacations in Montreat, North Carolina (Presbyterian heaven for those who have been there), where her family has a summer home. Amy's hobbies include camping, hiking, volleyball, kayaking, and spending time with her new husband, Jeffery.

Jennifer McBride

Jennifer grew up on the campus of the Baylor School, a private boarding and day high school in Chattanooga, Tennessee where her father taught for almost thirty years and where her family lived and participated in the boarding community. At present, she is a PhD candidate at the University of Virginia, pursuing a degree in theology and society and working for the Project on Lived Theology. After graduating in 1999 from the University of North Carolina at Chapel Hill, Jenny continued her academic pursuits as a Falls Church Fellow, engaging in theological study and social activism. During the Fellows program and the year thereafter, she worked full time at The Southeast White House, a community house in southeast Washington, D. C. Jenny is active at Christ Episcopal Church in Charlottesville, Virginia.

Clint McCann

Clint is Evangelical Professor of Biblical Interpretation at Eden Theological Seminary in St. Louis, Missouri. He is an ordained minister in the Presbyterian Church (USA), and served as a pastor for ten years before beginning to teach at Eden in 1987. He is the author of numerous articles and several books, including the Psalms commentary in *The New Interpreter's Bible*, Vol. 4 (Abingdon, 1996); Judges in the Interpretation commentary series (John Knox, 2002); and *Facing the Music: Faith and Meaning in Popular Songs* (with Darrell Cluck and Catherine George; Chalice Press, 1999).

Beth Maynard

Beth is rector of the Church of the Good Shepherd in Fairhaven, Massachusetts. Her publications include *Meditations for Lay Eucharistic Ministers, The Bread of Life,* (both from Morehouse), various sermons/articles, and *How to Evangelize a GenXer—NOT!* (from Forward Movement). She is a participant in U2 Internet fandom, a fledgling live show trader, and a contributor to "Drawing their Fish in the Sand," atu2.com's archive of U2 scripture references. She lives with her husband Mark Dirksen as close to the ocean as possible and does not own a Palm Pilot.

Shawnthea Monroe-Mueller

Shawnthea Monroe-Mueller, a native of South Dakota, was watching when MTV made its first appearance over twenty years ago. Raised outside of the church, she lists watching U2's video "Gloria" as one of her first spiritual experiences, or at least the moment Christianity began to look cool. A graduate of Yale Divinity School, Shawnthea now serves the First Congregational United Church of Christ in Moorhead, Minnesota. She lives in Fargo, North Dakota with her husband, Neil, and their three young children. Her dream project is an adult education series titled, "X-Files Theology: Trust God."

Stephen Butler Murray

Stephen is College Chaplain, Associate Director of the Intercultural Center, and Lecturer in Religion and Environmental Studies at Skidmore College in Saratoga Springs, New York. An ordained minister in the United Church of Christ, he has taught in the fields of theology and homiletics at Union Theological Seminary in and Auburn Theological Seminary and served previously as a parish minister in UCC and Lutheran churches. He earned the M.Div. at Yale University Divinity School and is a candidate for the PhD in systematic theology at Union Theological Seminary in New York.

Jamie Parsely

At press time, Jamie was looking forward to his ordination as a transitional deacon at Gethsemane Episcopal Cathedral in Fargo, North Dakota, where he serves on the pastoral team. He studied at the School of Theology at Thornloe University in Sudbury, Ontario, and St. Joseph's College in Standish, Maine. He also has an MFA in Creative Writing from Vermont College and is the author of four books of poems. His poems and fiction have been published in a wide variety of literary journals in the U.S. and Britain. He is also the editor of The Sheaf, the newspaper for the Diocese of North Dakota.

Eugene H. Peterson

Eugene lives and writes in Montana. He and his wife Janice have three children and six grandchildren. He holds degrees from Seattle Pacific University, New York Theological Seminary, and Johns Hopkins University. Ordained by the Presbyterian Church (USA), he was founding pastor of Christ Our King Presbyterian Church in Maryland where he served for 29 years, and following that was James Houston Professor of Spiritual Theology at Regent College in Canada for five years. His translation of the Bible, *The Message,* is quoted frequently by Bono.

Darleen Pryds

Darleen is assistant professor of spirituality and church history at the Franciscan School of Theology, which is a member of the Graduate Theological Union in Berkeley, California. Darleen is a Roman Catholic laywoman with a passion for lay preaching in the Roman Catholic tradition and for her beagle, Gracie, who makes her laugh everyday. She is author of several articles on the history of lay preaching and a book, *The King Embodies the Word: Robert d'Anjou and the Politics of Preaching* (Brill, 2000). Her forthcoming book is on a thirteenth-century adolescent street preacher, Rose of Viterbo.

Leslie Reinke

Leslie grew up in both the Dominican Republic (where his parents worked for many years as Christian ministers) and Canada. He came under the influence of U2's music in 1984. Leslie is employed in the high-tech sector but most days would rather spend time contemplating unanswerable questions. He adores his wife Kerri and their children Bethany and Lucian. Leslie enjoys many of the accoutrements of a twenty-first-century Western lifestyle but is serious about losing things that he cannot keep in order to gain what he can never lose.

Steve Stockman

The author of *Walk On: The Spiritual Journey of U2,* Steve is a regular speaker at Greenbelt, the biggest Christian arts festival in Europe. He also hosts his own radio show on BBC Radio Ulster, and his website, Rhythms Of Redemption (www.stocki.ni.org), is a popular stopping-off place for a variety of people who are interested in Christian faith and art. Currently Presbyterian chaplain at Queens University, Belfast, he has been quoting U2 for almost twenty years in sermons and articles. He married Janice in 1996 and they have two children, Caitlin and Jasmine Grace.

Henry VanderSpek

Henry has been on a journey of engaging culture and faith in many different ways. He has led student groups overseas with Inter-Varsity Christian Fellowship (IVCF) of Canada, worked with refugees in downtown Toronto, and written and researched a video series for Immigration Canada. In his spare time he engages the weird world of pop culture. He loves the music of Johnny Cash, Bob Dylan, Ron Sexsmith, U2, and any other artist with soul. All of these experiences find their way into Henry's creative endeavours, which include short stories, poetry, and perhaps one day a novel. He lives with his wife, Suzi, in Toronto, Canada.

Derek Walmsley

Derek is 45 years old and vicar of a church in West Yorkshire, England. He has been ordained in the Church of England for eleven years, having previously been a computer systems designer. He has about 200 U2 CDs plus lots of vinyl. Several years ago he wrote and presented a youth event called "The Gospel According To U2," which featured large-screen video and a live band playing U2 songs. He sports a beard and a black woolly hat, and plays guitar, but admits that he's not quite as good as The Edge.

Brian Walsh

Brian is a Christian Reformed Campus Minister at the University of Toronto and adjunct professor of theology of culture at Wycliffe College. He has been writing on Christian faith and contemporary culture for many years now and is the coauthor of *The Transforming Vision: Shaping a Christian World View* (IVP, 1984) and *Truth is Stranger Than It Used to Be: Biblical Faith in a Postmodern Age* (IVP, 1996). He is also the author of *Subversive Christianity: Imaging God in a Dangerous Time* (Alta Vista College Press, 1994), as well as a number of articles on singer/songwriter, Bruce Cockburn. He lives in

Toronto with his wife, Sylvia Keesmaat, their three children, an organic garden, and a growing CD collection.

Raewynne J. Whiteley

Raewynne is vicar of Trinity Episcopal "Old Swedes" Church in Swedesboro, New Jersey. She has a PhD in Homiletics, and has had a number of articles and sermons published. A particular area of interest is preaching and GenXers, about which she has written and taught. She grew up (in Australia) hearing her brother's U2 records playing, and recently rediscovered their music; it has become a favorite source of reflection for sermons and teaching. She is a proud owner of a New Beetle, and keeps the CD changer full of U2 CDs.